WOMEN'S STUDIES
An Emerging Discipline

WOMEN'S STUDIES
An Emerging Discipline

Editor
A. SURYAKUMARI

GYAN PUBLISHING HOUSE
NEW DELHI-110 002

ISBN : 81-212-0457-7

Library of Congress Card No. 93-900308

Published in India by

Gyan Publishing House
5 Ansari Road
New Delhi - 110002

Printed at: Rajdhani Printers

FOREWORD

The present work is the result of a 3-day workshop on "Methodology for Women's Studies', conducted in Mother Teresa Women's University, Tamilnadu. Women's Studies, as an emerging discipline, contain many pertinent issues relating to women in particular and society in general. These need to be resolved in the proper perspective, to provide the much needed direction, for women's welfare and empowerment, today and tomorrow. Research studies give promise of such a possibility. Research methods relating to Social Sciences, till 1986, have predominantly made use of quantitative techniques, which help to interpret data in qualitative form. But between the interpretations and the reality of situations, gaps appear to misinterpret facts. The qualitative methods of research are hence attempted, and this includes participatory methods, Content Analysis, Case Study, Observation and several others.

Research Methods for Women's Studies find ample relevance here. An introduction to Women's Studies—methodology is attempted through the papers, presented in this book. More rigorous work needs to be done and is awaited with eagerness.

As a new emerging area, women's studies as a discipline focuses on theory-building and theory-interpretation. These should not be misconstrued as methodology-based interpretations. Hence, much research has to be done in this direction, before effective methodology for such a research could be spelt out clearly.

As a first book, it is a good attempt. The several departments in the Women's University are planning to evolve meaningful methodology for Women's Studies research.

My best wishes for the pioneers.

S. Lakshmi

historical data. He suggested that a search for new kinds of sources, oral history, autobiographical writings, literary texts and archaeological artifacts should be found and new ways of interpretations of data have to be developed to integrate women into History and not merely construct a narrative of women in History. He further added that research needs to focus on issues relating to women and their interaction with the productive process rather than dealing merely with women's issues. He stressed that the true purpose and aim in writing women's History is to explore structures of oppression and exploring will help eradicating them.

Dr. Kumkum Roy in her paper, "The Challenge of Women's History" clearly indicated how the study of past will help in understanding the sources of women's oppression and their eradication. She quoted many a research work and discussed how they dealt with women's oppression and analysed the variety of forms in which women's resistance to and against the situation in which they were placed. She made clear the potentials inherent in reconstructing women's History and suggested that we should accept the challenges in recovering our past in all its complexity; it is also likely that more questions will emerge, more theoretical refinements will be possible and history in general will be enriched. She emphasised that in order to make this endeavour a success, we must be prepared to question many if not all of the accepted assumptions of our discipline, the definition of what is regarded as historically significant and at the same time test our new formulations against as wide a base of evidence as possible, recognising in particular the validity of the experiences of women no matter how diverse they may be.

Dr. Susie Jacob Tharu in her paper, "Towards a Historiography of Women in People's Struggles : Some questions arising from a study of women in the Telangana People's Movement of the 1940's" explained the role of women in Telangana movement.

On the whole the papers which one solicited specifically

for the workshop are multifaceted explaining various conceptual frameworks for research on Women's Studies.

I am especially grateful to our former Vice-Chancellor, Dr. Jaya Kothai Pillai for her unstinting support and encouragement, and for providing funds needed for this workshop. I would like to express my gratitude and sincere thanks to our present Vice-Chancellor Dr. S. Lakshmi, for writing the Foreword to this work. I am deeply indebted to Dr. Maithreyi Krishnaraj, SNDT Women's University, Bombay and Dr. C.S. Lakshmi, free-lance writer for helping me in the plan of the workshop. My sincere thanks are due to all my colleagues: Dr. Devadatta, Prof. of Tamil, Dr. Mary Josephine Louis, Prof. of Education, and my colleagues in the Department Dr. P.N. Premalatha, Ms. P.V. Manoraujitham, Dr. G.A.L. Satyarani, Dr. K.S. Rema Devi, Ms. Zubaida Hussaini and Ms. Rajeswari for extending a helping hand in making the workshop a fruitful one.

A. SURYAKUMARI

PREFATORY NOTE

Dr. Neera Desai

Women's Studies is in great demand by a few academicians from outside the system. With a lot of legitimisation, Women's Studies would be important to the non-academic people also. With our constant and vigilant effort we can make Women's Studies an instrument for social transformation. Thus, Women's Studies is not another irrelevant social science. It is an academic action. Women's Studies is a bi-discipline or multi-discipline or cross disciplined subject.

Women's Study is very important because the tendency of women's dreams are not considered. We are giving legitimacy to the experience and problems of Women's Studies. When we talk of methodology, it includes both perspective and usage of doing research. The methodology should focus attention on women over the centuries. Women's problems, constraints etc. are not taken into consideration. Our aim is to break the women's forced silence. Silence is the switch which was entrusted to her. The shell has to be broken and women must become visible. To bring out the woman from her invisibility is a different kind of work and for this a different sort of methodology should be evolved. There is one methodology through which the total picture of women is available. One of the most important requirements of Women's Studies research is sensitiveness.

Sensitiveness, subjectivity and value free perspective are the three important aspects in Women's Studies. We are progressing in Women's Studies in India. We should compare it with what is happening in other Asian countries. On the main stream it is a soft subject and when we study that discipline, it means we are enriching it.

CONTRIBUTORS

Dr. Neera Desai is at present an Emeritus Professor of Sociology at SNDT Women's University, Bombay, and Women's Studies scholar of international repute. She was the Founder Director of the Research Centre for Women's Studies (1977-1986) Bombay, the first such Centre to be established in the country. She has many contributions to her credit and holds many academic positions. She has done much to promote Women's Studies in India through her own work as well as through assistance to other centres and scholars. She is author and co-author of a number of books. Prominent among them are *Women in Modern India* (1st edn : 1957), *Women and Society in India* with Maithreyi Krishna Raj, *Indian Women : Change and Challenge in the International Decade 1975-1985* with Vibhuti Patel and recently she has edited a book on *A Decade of Women's Movement in India.* Her research interests are focussed on sociology of the family, women's movements and women and the media.

Dr. Uma Chakravarthy is a feminist historian. She is working at Miranda College for women, Delhi and has been teaching since 23 years. Her Ph.D. thesis is on Buddhism which was published recently. Her specialization is social History. Her articles, *The Sita Myth* and *The Rise of Buddhism as Experienced by Women* are contributions worth noting in the field of women's studies.

Dr. Aparna Basu had done her Ph. D. from Cambridge University, England, and her Dissertation is on the *Growth of*

Education and Political Development in India 1898-1920. At present she is Professor, of History, University of Delhi, Delhi. Her specializations are history of education and women's history. She has been a university teacher for 30 years and has done a great deal to promote Women's Studies in India through her projects, "Three Generations of Gujarat Women", and "Women's Education 1845-1947: Selection of Documents". She is the Associate Editor of *The Indian Economic and Social History Review,* a reputed journal on Indian History. Her publications are *Growth of Education and Political Development in India, 1898-1920,* (Delhi, 1974) and *Essays in the History of Education.*

Dr. Malavika Karlekar is a Senior Fellow at the Centre for Women's Development Studies, New Delhi. Basically, a sociologist – she has earlier taught Sociology at the University of Delhi and done a major research study on "Sweeper Women in Delhi". She has published *Poverty and Women's Work* (1982), and "Education and Inequality", in Andre Betielle (ed) *Equality and Inequality* (1983). Her current interests include teaching and curriculum preparation for Women's Studies, in addition to other research.

Dr. Prabha Mahale has been teaching Anthropology for past 16 years at Karnataka University. She has also taught for two years at the Queen's University, Northern Ireland. Though, originally, her specialization was Educational Anthropology, her current interest and focus of research is on Women's Studies. She is engaged in organizing a series of seminars, talks and conferences on Women's Studies at the University. As a member of the Federation of Voluntary Organizations in Karnataka she has worked for the training programme for women field workers in rural development and is also working as a resource person for voluntary organizations working for rural and tribal development. She is a member of the Karnataka State Social Welfare Advisory Board.

Dr. P. Sudhir is Reader in History, University of Hyderabad. He has done Ph. D. from the School of Oriental and

African Studies, London on "British Attitudes to Indian Nationalism, 1922-1935". He has presented papers at various seminars on different aspects of imperialism and modern history. His areas of research interest are modern Indian history and women's history.

Dr. Kumkum Roy teaches History in Satyawati Co-educational College of Delhi University. She is a feminist historian and along with Dr. Uma Chakravarthy has written articles on women's history.

Dr. Susie Jacob Tharu is working as Reader in the Central Institute of English and Foreign Languages, Hyderabad. She has published various articles and papers related to Women's Studies. Her research area of specialization is women's history.

Dr, V. Yashoda Devi, the first lady D. Litt. from the University of Madras, has been the Principal of Mahila Vidhyalaya and Lecturer and Reader at Sri Venkateswara University. She is the author of *History of Andhra Country, 1000 A.D.—1500 A.D.*

CONTENTS

CHAPTER ONE

Beyond the Altekarian Paradigm : Towards a New Understanding of Gender Relation in Early Indian History

DR. UMA CHAKRAVARTI

Discussion on the status of women has a unique position in the writing, teaching, and learning of early Indian history. Further, some of the conclusions of this discussion have actually found their way into the syllabi of school and undergraduate courses. For whatever it is worth, there is some information on women in almost every text book on ancient India. This kind of information does not occur in any other course of history since there has been no tradition of a separate discussion on the status of women. The uniqueness of the situation made its point while I was correcting examination papers some time ago. A question on the main features of later Vedic civilization resulted in a spate of answers dealing with the position of women. It was clear that to most students one of the important indices of a civilization was the position that women occupied in it. This general understanding is based on an informal debate that took over 150 years to crystallise and percolate down to a large number of people among the upper classes in India.

The existing material on women in early India, however, has a seriously limiting dimension to it, especially when we consider the negative effect that such work has had on a real understanding of women in history. It might therefore be worth-while to explain why the first historians undertook studies of the status of women, why these remained confined essentially to Ancient India and also review the state of the existing literature so that one may be able to evaluate the worth of the available studies. This will, in turn, help us to outline the kind of work that needs to be done in the future.

The women's question took a central place in the early stages of the national movement. The socio-religious reform movements of the 19th century advocated a reform of Hindu society whose twin evils were seen as the existence of caste and the low status of women. All the major reformers of the time attacked the practice of Sati, child marriage and enforced widowhood, and this was a common platform whether the reformers belong to the Brahmo Samaj in Bengal, the Prarthana Samaj in Maharashtra or the Arya Samaj in Northern India. The pre-occupation with these questions was derived, at least in part, from the dominance of Sanskritic models in the 19th century, since the major thrust in the debate came from within the upper sections of the Hindu community. The above mentioned characteristic has survived in the women's question even in contemporary times, where the study of the identity of women is based almost entirely on Sanskritic models and the myths conditioning women.

Another feature which had significant consequences for the general debate on the status of women is that both the proponents of the reform as well as the opponents of the reform looked back to the ancient texts as the source from which both groups took their positions and invoked the sanctions of the Shashtras in putting forward their arguments. This naturally necessitated a study of the position of women over the course of history. The deciding factor in the debate between the liberals or progressives and the conservatives was the relative antiquity of the source from which they were quoting. The older the source, the more authentic and authoritative it was considered. Raja Ram Mohan Roy, Ishwarchandra Vidyasagar and R.G. Bhandarkar all quoted copiously from the Sanskrit sources in order to attack the conservatives. There is thus a direct corelation between the concerns of the Brahmo Samaj, Arya Samaj, and the Prarthana Samaj and the writings on the position of women in Hindu civilization.

Since the traditional work on the status of women in India exists entirely within the context of Hinduism, it is heavily pre-occupied with religious and legal questions such as the right to widow re-marriage, the existence of the institution of Niyoga, the right to property for women, the origin and development of the institution of *stridhana,* the right of the childless widow to adopt and so on. On the religious front there is an obession with the right of a woman to perform religious sacrifices either by herself or with her husband, as also with her interest and involvement with the pursuit of religious goals. The social position of women is usually concerned with the inclusion or exclusion of women in public assemblies and their right to education. On the whole, the perspective on women is confined to seeing them within the context of the family. It is this status of women within the family, and primarily in the relationship of wives to husbands with which the traditional writers were concerned.

Another feature of the traditional writing on the position of women is that they were based entirely on Brahmanical sources. Even if these sources are considered to be reasonably authentic, which I have reason to doubt, they carry the problem of (a) an inherent bias of the *brahmanas* (b) reflecting the precepts of the *brahmanas* rather than the actual practice of the people and (c) confining themselves with the upper castes. At best, the existing work can be termed as a partial view from above. How unsatisfactory such unconditional reliance upon Brahmanical sources has been, will be clear further on in this paper.

The analysis of the position of women in Ancient India has also been coloured by the fact that almost all the works have been written by scholars who would fall within the Nationalist school of history. Writing at a time when Hindu social institutions were being subjected to fierce criticism by a generation that was imbibing western education and western values, these scholars worked hard to show that the position of women had been high in the ancient past. The contemporary evils reflecting the low position of women were responsible for the Hindu sense of inferiority in relation to their ruling masters. As a reaction, Hindu scholars argued that the evils were only a temporary aberration and could easily be eliminated. The general thrust of the work has therefore been to demonstrate that the status of women was very high in the Vedic period ; according to this view there was a general decline which later reached a rock bottom level with the coming of the invaders, especially the Muslims, who abducted Hindu women and violated them, and these circumstances resulted in the development of such evils as Purdah, Sati, and female infanticide. This view has become widely prevalent since it appears regularly in popular literature and vernacular journals but we must point out that it is only an extension of traditional academic research.

Here is a fairly representative example from the open of a women scholar :

> "The tentl and the eleventh centuries saw the advent, and ater, the firm establishment of Muhammadans in this country. When Hindu culture came into clash with a culture far different from it's own, the leaders of society began to frame rules and laws to safeguard their interest-specially the position of women. Rigorous restrictions were placed on them...We find at this stage child marriage firmly enforced The death of a widow was preferred to her falling into evil hands. Hence, self-immolation of a widow was enjoined by the law Codes giving the unfortunate victim the hope of heavenly bliss. Such and several other customs were introduced which curbed the freedom of women to a very large extent. This was done perhaps to save her from the foreigners and to preserve the purity of the race." (Shakuntala Rao Shastri, *Women in the Sacred Laws*—pp. 172-173; & 189).

Similarly R.C. Dutt, the well-known nationalist historian and the first to present a coherent account of ancient Indian civilisation and of women, writes :

> "Absolute seclusion and restraint (of women) were not Hindu customs. They were unknown in India till Mohommedan times ..No ancient nation held their women in higher honour than the Hindus..." (pp. 168-169).

Such a sweeping view is untenable if one looks at the past without the tinted spectacles of the present. Even if one were to confine one' self to Brahmanical sources, there is enough evidence to show that women of the upper castes did not have access to the public domain by the early centuries of the Christian era, and that Manu and other law givers recommended early marriage for girls. Sati itself was associated with women of the ruling classes as is evident from the 7th century account of Harsha's early career. The structure of institutions that ensured the subordination of women was complete in all essentials long before the Muslims, as a religious community, had even come into being. The Muslim bogey was a convenient peg to explain the origin of all oppressive practices. It was particularly convenient for those who did not wish to see the structural framework of institutions that governed gender relations in early India mainly because it was the same framework that governed, women even in contemporary society. The term "patriarchy" was hardly used and even when it did stray into an occasional historian's writing it was a neutral term, completely divested of the power factor inherent in it; successfully depoliticised it lost its real importance.

The cultural encounter between England and India in the 19th century, which was the context for the emergence of nationalist historiography, shaped the focus and the thrust of writing on women in early India. The injury to the Hindu sense of superiority resulting from the unfavourable comparison between Hindu women and western women, which was common throughout the cultural encounter, was so marked that it frequently led to an inversion of the Vincent Smith syndrome. Vincent Smith's attitude was a general contempt for everything Indian. If he was faced with visual and incontrovertible proof of something worthwhile in Indian culture he would immediately attribute it to Greek influence. Historians writing on the position of women in ancient India reversed the argument by invariably trying to point out that nowhere else in the ancient world were women held in such high regard as in the India of 3000 years ago. They specially revelled in comparisons with Greece and Rome as in the passage below.

> "The historian of India who has studied the literature of the ancient Hindus will have no hesitation in asserting that never in the most polished days of Greece and Rome were women held in such high regard in those countries as in India three thousand years ago.'" (R.C. Dutt, p. 171).

Similarly, Altekar surveys the condition of women in ancient Greece, Rome and, Palestine and then reiterates that the position which women occupied at the dawn of civilisation during the Vedic age was much better (p. 337).

The need of the nationalist historians to resurrect examples of the lost glory of Indian womanhood has led to a selective focus on certain aspects of the ancient texts. This has often led to a sanitised interpretation of events, best illustrated by the nationalist rendering of the Gargi-Yajnavalkya debate, the most celebrated example of women's learning. The highlight of the account in Shakuntala Rao Shastri's book is the way the debate concludes. Gargi's questions to Yajnavalkya have by this time become more subtle and pointed. Yajnavalkya however clearly has no intention of allowing Gargi to win the prize of a thousand cows. At this stage of the debate he arbitrarily threatens Gargi with dire consequences if she persists in questioning him and so eliminates her from the contest. Despite this Shakuntala Rao Shastri sums up the episode without pointing to the unfairness of this clearly memorable confrontation between two Philosophers, one a man and another a woman. Instead she blithely states :

> "The persistent and obstinate enquiry of a woman brought forth the finest definition of the Supreme Reality. The motive of Gargi's enquiry was *not to test Yajnavalkya but to learn from him* (*Italics mine*) about the nature of Brahman." (p. 95).

Thus Gargi's fearlessness, independent mind and her ability to take on a well established philosopher is watered down in Rao Shastri's account; more importantly the unfairness of the contest is casually glossed over in order to present a picture of blissful, harmonious pursuit of philosophical truth.

The best known and most internally coherent nationalist work on women is Altekar's study on the position of women in Hindu civilization. His work is based primarily on Brahmanical sources and outlines the position of women from the earliest times right upto the mid-fifties of this century when the Hindu Code Bill was under consideration. Altekar's work represents the best that is available to us by way of Women's Studies in History but it also establishes very sharply the limitations of the traditional approach. Although the work unravles in details the entire body of opinion of the law makers on such areas as the education of women, marriage and divorce, the position of the widow, women in public life, proprietary rights of women, and the general position of women in society it is steeped in the nationalist understanding of the women's question. Further, his overwhelming concern is with women in the context of the family and one almost gets the feeling that the status of women needs to be raised in order to ensure the healthy development of the future race of India. In this he was reflecting the opinion of nationalist writers from the second half of the 19th century who placed tremendous importance on the physical regeneration of the Hindus.

A survey of Altekar's work will indicate the limitations inherent in his approach. His theoretical framework is spelt out in the very first page of his work. According to him :

> "One of the best ways to understand the spirit of a civilization and to appreciate its excellences and realise its limitations is to study the history of the position and status of women in it...The marriage laws and customs enable us to realise whether men regarded women as market commodities or war prizes or whether they realised that the wife is after all her husband's valued partner whose co-operation was indispensible for *happiness* and *success* in family life", (*Italics mine*) (p. 1.)

Altekar's own genuine commitment to reforming womeu's status led him into sometime making quaint statements which he intended as positive and progressive. Thus he suggests that although,

> "Women have low fighting value they have potential military value. By giving birth to sons they contribute indirectly to the fighting strength and efficiency of their community". (p. 3)

Further Altekar's programme for wom‹‐, despite his apparent liberality and sympathy for them was to view women primarily as stock breeders of a strong race. This view is particularly noticeable in his suggestions about women's education. In Altekar's programme of reform women were to be educated enough but in doing so one had to ensure that no undue strain was placed upon them. He expressed his fears thus :

> "As things stand today, girls have to pass the *same* examinations as boys and to learn housekeeping at home as well, all the while having less physical strength than their brothers. This certainly puts too much strain upon them and is *injurious to the future well-being of the race*". (*Italics mine*) (p. 28.)

Establishing the high status of women was the means by which 'Hindu' civilisation could be vindicated. This was the finished version of the nationalist answer to James Mill's denigration of Hindu civilisation published a century ago ; the locus of the barbarity of Hindu civilisation in James Mill's work (*A History of British India*) had lain in the abject condition of Hindu women. By reversing the picture Altekar was attempting to lay Mill's ghost aside. But it was easier to provide a general picture than to deal with a variety of customs oppressing women that still obtained in the early twentieth century. Altekar was thus forced to provide explanations for existing biases against women. For example he attempts to explain the Hindu preference for a son over a daughter by advancing a psychological argument as in the passage below :

> "If a cruel fate inflicted widowhood upon the daughter, the calamity would break the parent's heart. Remarriage being no longer possible, parents had to see the heart-rending pain of seeing their daughter wasting herself in interminable widowhood...parents had often to pass through the terrible ordeal of seeing their daughter's burning themselves alive on the funeral pyre of their husbands. To become a daughter's parent thus became a source of endless worry and misery...As a natural consequence...passages about the undesirability of the birth of daughter become more numerous". (p. 5.)

Altekar is particularly weak in his attempts at relating the status of women at a given point of time with social organization as a whole. Thus early Vedic society which did not as yet have noticeable concentration of power, or a well developed institution of kingship, is the context for Altekar's unnecessary explanation for the absence of queens. Since Altekar is convinced about the high status of women in the Vedic period, he feels he has to account for the reason why we do not hear of women as queens. Thus he is constrained to suggest that,

> "Aryans were gradually establishing their rule in a foreign country surrounded on all sides by an indigeneous hostile population that considerably out

numbered them. Under such circumstances queens ruling in their own rights or as regents were *naturally unknown*." (*Italics mine*) (p. 339).

Similarly Altekar has a facile explanation as to why women did not own property. According to him,

> "Landed property could be owned only by one who had the power to defend it against actual or potential rivals and enemies. Women were obviously unable to do this and so could hold no property". (p. 339).

In his inability to see women within a specific social organisation and recognising patriarchal subordination of women Altekar was not unique. Like other he was reflecting a deeply internalised belief in biological determinism and therefore in the physical inferiority of women.

Very occasionally however Altekar shows flashes of insight into the socio-economic context within which women's subordination was achieved. For example in his analysis of the causes for the 'fall' of the status of the Aryan woman Altekar suggests a connection with the subjugation of the Sudras as a whole. He argues that the Aryan conquest of the indigeneous population and its loose incorporation as members of a separate *varna* had given rise to a huge population of semi-servile status. In such a situation Aryan women ceased to be producing members of society and thus lost the esteem of society. But even as he makes this broadly contextual explanation, Altekar is insensitive to the crucial distinction between the participation of women as *producers* and participation in terms of *controlling production*. Thereafter Altekar's semihistorical insight is unfortunately lost and popular prejudice takes over. Like the ancient Brahmanical law givers he appears to have a horror of Sudra women as in this passage :

> "The introduction of the non-Aryan wife into the Aryan household is the *Key* (Italics mine) to the gradual deterioration of the position of women...

> The non-Aryan wife with her ignorance of Sanskrit language and Hindu religion could *obviously not enjoy the same religious privileges as the Aryan consort* (*Italics mine*).
> Association with her must have tended to affect the purity of speech of the Aryan co-wife as well. Very often the non-Aryan wife may have been the favourite one of her husband, who may have often attempted to associate her with his religious sacrifices in preference to her better educated but less loved Aryan co-wife. This must have naturally led to grave mistakes and anomalies in the performance of the ritual which must have shocked the orthodox priests ..Eventually it was felt that the object could be gained by declaring the whole class of women to be inteligible for Vedic Studies and religious duties". (pp. 345-46).

This facile argument was in Altekar's view the key factor in the decline in the status of women. Altekar is completely obtuse to other historical explanations. The possibility that the Sudra woman, whom he regards as a threat, could have contributed to a more dynamic and active kind of womanhood for Hindu society would not even occur to Altekar because his focus is on Aryan women (regarded them as the progenitors of the upper caste women of Hindu society) and in his racist view, Sudra women counted for nothing. The most important consequence of Altekar's limited repertoire of biological and psychological explanations was that the logic of the distorted social relations between men and women is completely obscured. The kind of explanations offered by Altekar might appear to be astoundingly trivial to us today but it is important to remember that, by and large, nationalist historians were content to restrict historical explanations to cultural factors while writing about ancient India. This was in contrast to their focus on economic and social factors while discussing British Rule in India.

In summing up nationalist historiography on women in early India we might draw attention to the fact that the

Altekarian paradigm, though limiting and biased, continues to nevertheless influence and even dominate historical writings. In essense what emerges from the mass of detail he accumulated is the construction of a picture of the idyllic condition of women in the Vedic age. It is a picture which now pervades the collective consciousness of the upper castes in India and has virtually crippled the emergence of a more analytically rigorous study of women in ancient India. There is thus an urgent need to move forward and rewrite history, a history that does justice to women by examining social processes and the structures they create thus crucially shaping and conditioning the relations between men and women. Just as Altekar displaced Mill in his work, it is time we realised that despite Altekar's substantial contribution we must lay his ghost aside and begin afresh.

CHAPTER TWO

Methodology in Women's History—An Intergenerational Study of a Family

DR. APARNA BASU

It is well known that women receive little or no attention in traditional history writing. Even among radical or socialist histories they are all too often mentioned as an after-thought, if at all; tagged on, rather than present in their own right. Women's history still has to be argued for. Not only political but even social and economic historians have left out women. Working class has generally meant working men; women are wives, mother and daughters of working men. Domestic life is treated as a static unchanging backcloth to the world of real historical activity. Women are peripheral both to production and to the class struggle. Neglect of women has, I think led to the impoverishment of social history. Men and women do inhabit different worlds with boundaries which have been defined by men-the public world of men and the private world of women, work and home. Exploring the relationship between these two worlds will enrich all social history.

Women's history began as an act of reclamation. Its progress has been charted in the successive titles carried by some of the leading publications in the field. Woman has been hidden from history,[1] the aim was to have *Clio's*

Consciousness raised[2] by *liberating women's history*[3] from ignorance and neglect, and in the resulting work, women in history are becoming visible[4].

Our view of the past has become dramatically widened in scope in the last few years. We have become aware of historical problems and issues of whose existence we were previously oblivious of. In the study of Indian nationalism, for instance, we have 'discovered' the role of poor peasants, tribals and now women-suppressed groups, whose contribution had previously been ignored. This is a considerable achievement.

In our efforts to recover and understand the past, we must place women, not in isolation but as part of the totality, For instance, Gail Malmgreen's interesting and well informed study on the emergence of utopian feminist ideas and their reception among the British working class, provides a useful lesson of how detailed knowledge of British labour history is a pre-requisite to the understanding of women's place in the socialist movement[5]. Similarly, Patricia Hollis' *Women in public, 1850-1950, Documents of the Victorian Women's Movement,*[6] shows awareness of the general historical context. Women's history has to be related with social, political and economic history. This does not mean that women's history should simply conform to standards and criteria of existing historical scholarship, women's history should try to enlarge and alter it, transcending the limits of 'conventional' history and confront historians with new questions which they have so far ignored. But at the same time, women's historians must also take 'Conventional' history seriously to do justice to their own field and succeed in making an impact on history teaching and research.

We have to restore women to her rightful place in history and explore the meanings of women's unique historical experience. The real women in history have to emerge, beyond defication and vilification. We have to see women as a force in politics, as reformers, revolutionaries, searching for an identity in their nation, their class, themselves. Women as producers, as peasants, as workers, artisans, domestic servants in their roles as wives, daughters and mothers have to become visible.

Women's history is developing into a new research area at a particularly exciting time. It has been stimulated by two related but essentially independent developments, the maturation of social history and the appearance of a renewed women's movement. In India, it is only since the 1970s, after the publication of the *Report of the Committee on the Status of Women in India* that scholars have become aware of the under assessment in social studies of women's role and inputs.

In seeking to add women to the fund of historical knowledge, women's history has revitalized theory for it has shaken the conceptual foundations of historical study. It has done this by making problematical three of the basic concerns of historical thought : periodisation, the categories of historical analysis and theories of social change. Women's history is emerging as a vital field of historical enquiry and has raised broad conceptual and methodological issues.

Women's history is a relatively new area of research in India. I have done a study which investigates a relatively unexplored area of the Indian women's world and aims at filling up a lacuna in our existing knowledge of society.

This study is an attempt to understand the changing life patterns and consciousness of middle class urban women in Gujarat. It focuses on four generations of women in my family to study the process of social change, the continuities and discontinuities in their lives. In a broader sense this spans about a hundred years—1870s-1970s of the social history of Gujarat. Vidyagauri Nalkanth, my grandmother, was a pioneer in many fields : the first women graduate of Gujarat, she was an eminent social reformer who throughout her life was actively associated with numerous women's educational, social and philanthropic organisations. Vidyagauri Nilkanth's family, both from her mother's side and her husband's was intimately involved in the social and religious reform movements of Gujarat.

Being part of the family, an insider, I had some distinct advantages and at the same time some disadvantages. The advantage was that I had a thorough knowledge of the history and cultural background of the family and intuitive sensitivity, empathy and understanding. I was familiar with the customs and the language. Members of the family possibly gave me more time than they would to an outsider and perhaps talked more frankly about their lives. There was the danger of course of not being dispassionate and objective-advantages an outsider would have.

A life history, as I am using the term here, embodies the story of a person's life constructed by the researcher from written records and oral accounts. A life history differs both from an autobiography, which is a first person written account of a person's own life and from a biography, which is a third person's written account of the subjects life. Life histories are an important tool for the social historian and are especially useful for studying the various types and sorts of people whose history would otherwise get lost. They are a source of factual data a base for generating hypotheses, testing theories and opening new enquiries along thematic lines. We will know very little in the future about the lives of most of the women alive in the world today without collecting their life histories. We can considerably improve our grasp of all sorts of history by collecting life histories.

Sociologists and historians have been concerned with the problem of change and continuity in the family structure and relationships and considerable work has been done at the macro level to see the inter-relationship between familial and societal charge. But good studies at the micro level are lacking. Change inevitably introduces the persepective of time and we need to know how things were at an earlier time in order to deduce the degree and direction of change at a later point in time. We lack reliable evidence of a systematic kind regarding the nature of Indian society and its institutions at an earlier point of time, say in the middle of the nineteenth century. We have discriptions of the ideal Hindu family, what relationships *ought* to be, but the failure to distinguish between normative, culturally prescribed patterns and actual empirical reality is a source of great deal of confusion. Factual evidence of how people actually behaved in the past is not easily available. This is where the historian can come in and help the sociologist by filling in the gaps. Vidyagauri's is a Hindu, urban, middle class, upper caste family. This study will, therefore, mainly throw light on changes among women in this category. This is not to suggest that other categories of women Muslim women, rural, working class or scheduled caste are any less important or that only the leadership elite deserve the focus. But in the context of certain historical developments in India, the women of the middle class have specific interesting problems which make the investigation worth undertaking. While it is true that women of different classes and castes often have antagonistic interests, it equally holds true that their problems as women cut across regional/cultural/caste barriers.

Methodology

The methodology adopted has been interdisciplinary, based on tools borrowed from the discipline of history, sociology, comparative literature and women's studies. The following sources have been used :

(i) Women's own writings, i.e. contributions to journals, memoirs, autobiographies, letters, private diaries. These reflect their own version of their ideas, hopes and self perceptions. Writings in women's journals are of special value as they provide an important means of communicating among women, while autobiographies, letters and diaries present an intimate picture of their recognition of their problems and view points. It is fortunate that women in this family have written about themselves, edited women's magazines and written women's columns in newspapers. (This approach is borrowed from the newly emerging discipline of women's studies).

(ii) Men in this family have also left behind written

records. Some of them have written on Women's issues also. These have been looked into, in order to assess the impact of male defined values of women.

(This has required borrowing methods from the 'history of ideas').

(iii) A number of in-depth personal interviews were done in order to obtain an insight into women's evaluation of their own lives and relationships and what changes they perceive in the present generation.

(This tool has been adopted from 'oral history')

(iv) A questionnaire was carefully prepared and not only women of the family concerned but a number of women in Ahmedabad who had the same kind of caste/class background were also interviewed.

(v) Contemporary creative literature in Gujarati-novels, essays, short stories were gleaned since they reflect prevailing/changing ideologies and customs.

(This method is one of the discipline of contemporary literature).

(vi) Archival material, government reports were also consulted.

(This is done according to traditional historical methodology).

(vii) Relevant published secondary books and articles in English and Gujarati were also examined.

Social forces play an important role in shaping individual life and character; consequently, important as life histories are, they must be seen in conjunction with the institutional and cultural changes in the background. Only in such combination can the full significance of life histories be understood and appreciated. Hence, this study relies partly on oral interviews and partly on written records.

Several methods have been devised by sociologists for studying family change. The inter-generational approach has been adopted here and the life histories of women in one family over three generations have been presented.

REFERENCES

1. Sheila Rowbotham, *Hidden from History, Three Hundred Years of Women's Oppression and the Fight Against It*, 1973.
2. M. Hartman and L. Banner (ed). *Clio's Consciousness Raised New Perspectives in the History of Women*, New York. 1974.
3. Bernice A. Carroll (ed), *Liberating Women's History* Illinois, 1976.
4. R. Bridenthal and C. Koonz (ed), *Becoming visible Women in European History*, Boston, 1977.
5. G. Malmgreen, *Neither Bread Nor Roses : Utopian Feminists and the English Working Class, 1800-1850*. London, 1978.
6. Patricia Hillis (ed) *Women in Public, 1850-1900. Documents of the Victiorian Women's Movement*, London, 1979.

CHAPTER THREE

Within the Zenana : Readings From "A Certain Housewife's Diary"

DR. MALAVIKA KARLEKAR

A common epistemological issue in the social sciences relates to definitions; invariably, there is more than one point of view, representing different schools of thought, according to the ideological prediliction of the author, his or her age and sex. This is particularly true of an amorphous area like Women's Studies. By and large, however, it is now accepted that Women's Studies aims at building up a body of knowledge based on the discovery, contemporary documentation and analysis of women's lives and their various roles. There is an increasing demand that we see meaning in what has been previously empty space.[1] This empty space was more often than not made up of women, toiling, scrubbing, cooking and even occasionally reading and writing. Little was known about them, and in any case not much significance was attached to their functions. The 'public' world of men, with its areas of decision-making, intrigue, influence and power, was regarded as primary and vital.

One of the primary aims of Women's Studies is to make women visible. It combines the purely archaeological exercise of digging out information on women buried deep in human history and writing with a continued impetus for more contemporary work. At the next stage, there is the need for an analysis of all the material thus unearthed or being generated. For, as "a critical instrument" in our understanding of society, its role in developing analytical and theoretical dimensions is not inconsequential[2]. The present essay attempts to combine archaeology with some analysis: through the reading of a diary of a Nineteenth Century Bengali housewife, we get insights into a fast-changing society and the extent to which women accepted or rejected the new roles being envisaged for them. In India, after the 1830s there was a growing awareness among a section of the emergent, Western-educated middle class of the need to educate their womenfolk. For instance, the professional middle class in Bengal[3] was greatly influenced by the Victorian model of happy domesticity based on the educated women as helpmate, sympathetic mother, companion, friend and so on. While the girls schools did not gain ground until almost the end of the century *Zenana* education acquired respectability much sooner. Under this system. girls and women (many of whom were married) were tutored within the home either by English Missionary women or India converts. Pupils were taught individually or in small groups in accordance with a syllabus regarded as suitable for women from respectable homes. The stress was on fluency in language and literature, with primary emphasis on Bengali and on some simple English, a little Geography, History, Elementary Arithmetic and etiquette, sewing, knitting and embroidery. The learning of science and Mathematics beyond a certain level was generally eschewed. It was not unusual for men to teach their wives, sisters and daughters at night or in the early hours of the day. This was either in addition to formal tuition or as an alternative to it. Through these means it was hoped that women would adjust better to the new ideas and influences emerging from the West.

By and large, the impact of the social reform movement-and I am using the term to encompass changes not only in social customs but also to the introduction of education and a new style of life-has been viewed a beneficial and liberating for those concerned. However, there has been little attempt to look at the point of view of those affected more closely. In part, the tendency to rely on secondary sources may be explained in terms of a methodological preference, however, of greater importance are the implications of the assumption that directed change is by definition beneficent. This assumption may be perfectly valid; what is less easily acceptable is the political motive of introducing change on the basis of a partial assessment of the affected groups. Such an attitude is a reflection of an entire ideological position where interpretation of the needs of an under-privileged, relatively powerless or supposedly unenlightened group is worked upon by the more powerful and liberated. In his well-known exposition entitled *Orientalism*, Edward said has explained how the Occidental ruler viewed the subordinate Oriental. In fact, "European culture gained in strength and identity by setting itself off against the Orient as a sort of surrogate or even underground self[4]". Borrowing from Said, I would say that from the mid-19th century onwards not only the colonial ruler, but also the archetypal Bengali middle class gentleman, steeped through Western education in values of rationality, empiricism and scientism adopted a similar approach to those who according to him, were floundering in ignorance and intellectual poverty. In particular, he directed his attention gradually to women. There was a fairly strict pattern of segregation within the home. with separate women's quarters. Physical segregation was also marked by the evolution of separate women's sub-cultures.

Often changes were introduced in the lives of middle class Bengali women, in many cases really without understanding fully what was being changed or accepting that it was not difficult to throw the baby out with the bath water, the overweaning blanket assumption was that women's lives were in need of immediate reform. It is undoubtedly true that in Bengal administrative and legislative decisions improved considerably the status of women through the banning of Sati, child marriage and encouraging widow remarriage; at the same time, men appeared to have little comprehension of the principles of organisation, hierarchy and internal rules which characterised the separate world of women. Like the Occidental scholar, they formed judgements on the basis of inadequate or faulty information and proceeded to advocate reforms for all.

The advocacy of education for women had two aims; the first was the overt one of providing emergent Bengali middle class society with women acculturated in Victorian values and second, through this process, women were firmly brought within the ambit of the male world and value system. For many women who emerged from the confines of the female world, their first teachers were fathers, brothers and husbands. It would not be out of place to point out that male apprehensions-if not fear-of female powers[5] characterised many responses to the separate women's world. Effortlessly such apprehensions were translated into denigrations of this world as mystical, non-rational and unenlightened; it thus became that much easier to speak of the need for change in the women's realm with its distinct culture and norms. Such interventions, were, for obvious reasons, based on a limited understanding of reality, and lead to the creation of an ideal in keeping with the needs of male society. The perpetuation of this ideal has in fact resulted in the educational stereotyping of girls, the influence of which continues to the present day.

Thus, when the history of Nineteenth Century Bengal was written or thought about, it routinely took into consideration the point of view of the upper caste, middle class man or the *Bhadralok*[6] who has benefitted greatly from colonial rule. Literally translated to mean "gentlemen", or "gentlemen", (the same word encompassing both the singular as well as the plural) this term as also *bhadra samaj* or the society of the civilised, symbolised an entire new way of life; urbanisation, proliferating white collar jobs in the professions and in the many offices suited the rulers as much as it did the newly emergent middle class. Competition, both for a limited number of jobs and with respect to the emulation of the right style of life also brought with it groupism. It would be more apt to describe the *bhadralok* as a conglomeration of several subgroups rather than as a homogenous category. The foundation for occupational mobility was laid by a fast-expanding educational system where the school replaced the indigenous *pathshala* or primary school. The need for educating girls and women arose out of a wider commitment to learning in general: for the *bhadralok*, knowledge was sacred. In no time, large sections took avidly to the new institutions emanating from the West. The new middle classes became ardent worshippers at the feet of the goddess of rational, positivistic thought.

By the second half of the last century Bengali women started writing about themselves as well as noting down their responses to the changing environment. In many cases, their point of view was quite different from that of men, or the ideas put forth of them by men. In recent years, the need to understand Indian history from the view point of the subaltern which is an attribute of subordination expressed "in terms of class, caste, age, gender and office" has resulted in several useful case studies of peasant consciousness, *adivasi* uprisings, trade union organisation and agrarian tensions.[7] In doing so, these historians have provided insights into how non-elitist, underprivileged groups perceived their existence. Though the middle class educated Bengali *bhadramahila* or lady was, in absolute terms privileged, she was clearly under privileged *vis-a-vis* and *bhadralok*. Her inferior position arose out of her sex and of the subordinate role assigned to her within the family. Further, with the incorporation of women in the man's world of learning where, nonetheless, knowledge was selectively disseminated, inequality at home was matched by inequality in access to education. In most accounts written of the period, women are mentioned fleetingly, if at all, the assumption being that they benefitted greatly from the changes introduced in their lives. It was not until recently that an attempt has been made to look at women's response to the situation[8].

Feminist literary criticism has been increasingly concerned with the presence of the male voice in women's writings. In the present context, literacy and learning for women meant acquiring the ability to use a male-dominated language which has its differences with the languages of the *antahpur*. Literally translated to mean "inner house", the *antahpur* represented both the physical separation of the women's quarters as well as symbolically characterised a different world from that of men. The original users of the written word were men who had not only written most of the texts in use but also in some cases given guidance on the interpretation of discourse. Women who were being educated had to adjust to a degree of psychological and intellectual manipulation; it thus becomes important to ascertain how they responded to the situation. Did they take on the male stereotypes of women and accept that they were helpless creatures in imminent need of redemption ? Or did women manage to retain an inherent sense of self which manifested itself through different forms of self-expression ? In other words, observers of women's participation in the male world of learning have been concerned with the domination or colonisation of the women's mind, and hence with the impact of writings, by those more powerful than herself; in most cases. living and inter-acting in an universe where relevant values, decision-making, modes of behaviour and interaction are determined and expounded upon by men, the women. enters into an essentially subordinate relationship with the opposite sex.

In their *The Mad women in the Attic*[9], feminist literary critics Sandra Gilbert and Susan Gubar discuss the idea of the pen being a metophorical penis : the author of a text "as a father, a progenitor, a procreator, an aesthetic patriarch whose pen is an instrument of a generative power like his penis"[10]. The male writer creates discourse, which then becomes his property. Historically, this was all the more easy as reading, writing and thinking were regarded as male activities; ' if male sexuality is integrally associated with the assertive presence of literary power female sexuality is associated with the absence of such power".[11] Right upto the Nineteenth Century, the creation of most women in literature was the monopoly of men. In so doing, the woman was "killed" into a "perfect" image of herself". The authors liken the creation of the faint, limp and malleable female to a killing of her and of her individuality. Her literary representation is basically an act of *reification*, a distancing from the flesh and blood reality.

It is ultimately left to the individual woman writer to deal with these stereotypes. She can overcome and contradict or choose to succumb and accept. In her influential and provocative essay entitled "professions for Women", Virginia Woolf commented on how it was essential for women who wished to write to first "kill" the phantom of the angel in the house "who used to come between me and my paper"[12]. In other words, in order to express themselves freely and honestly, women writers need to destroy and contradict the dominant stereotype of themselves as personifications of domesticated heavenly beings, through their writings they have to prove that they feel frustration and dissatisfaction wi h this idealisation. For underlying this idealisation is the deep-seated motive of freezing women into a mould of domesticity and submissiveness, so essential for the success of men in an increasingly competitive world. Further, women needed to show that the expression of emotions such as love, anger and hatred flowed as easily from their pens as it did from that of men. In so doing they would work against pervading and stultifying stereotypes. However, this independence of mind was not always easy to achieve.

With growing industrialisation and a cut-throat market economy, it suited the British middle class to reinforce, through various sources, the image of the female home-maker *par excellence*. By the middle of the Nineteen Century, the Bengali middle class too fast realised the merit of a sympathetic home environment based on the willing cooperation of the woman. In order to create this compliant and understanding woman and bring her away from the *antahpur* culture it was; as we shall see, essential for her to have the right kind of education. Thus learning and writing for women were primarily introduced for the creation of accomplished house-of power and control over the women and their development within a prescribed format. However, though men may have been the owners of what they wrote, they could neither control interpretations of their work nor fully monitor women's access to and use of literacy. While most women were duly grateful for being granted access (however limited) to the preserve of male power, a few used their skills to express themselves frankly on prevailing social injustices. Women wrote novels, essays and about themselves, providing valuable insights into their lives. The articulation of such views often acted as a cathersil, triggered by the unequal encounter between the sexes and between cultures.

Autobiographical writing is a literary genre of considerable importance to students of literature as well as to society. Over here. I am looking at it purely as data relevant for an understanding of a particular phase in the evolution of Bengali society. The desire as well as the ability to express oneself often coincides with a specific phase in the life cycle when the sense of personal identity and awareness of the self is heightened. Some autobiographies more than others give expression to the feelings and personalised responses of the authors to a particular situation or course of events; others are primarily a chronicle of events. Whatever its aim, writing about oneself results in soul-searching, a quest for the right statement of one's views and so on. For many Bengali women who felt the urge to write or talk about themselves, the desire came at a time when external factors were affecting family life; old tensions were giving way to new ones as many traditional relationships started changing, or they simply had more times as in widowhood and old age. In particular, with access to learning and writing women started examining hierarchical family relations and their own roles. They were helped by an ambience which increasingly stressed the need for social, physical and occupational mobility The East India Company and later, the British Empire, provided substantial scope for ambitious and adventurous men who wanted to be freed of the feudal frame of reference and complex family obligations.

In some cases, and this is particularly true of the autobiographical writings of women, the act of putting pen to paper or recounting one's existence is like a cry of anguish against a life of oppression. The dictated life of Sharadasundari Debi, mother of the eminent social reformer, Keshub Chunder Sen, is a long and sad narration of ill-treatment by her in-laws after her widowhood, at the age of nineteen.[13] Between 1876 and the 1970s, there is a record of at least fifty autobiographies and autobiographical sketches having been written by Bengali women. The earliest was by Rassundari Debi, the wife of an East Bengal *Zamindar*, who was born in 1811. Unlike many of those who followed her, the self-taught Rassundari received little encouragement from her family, and recounted how she used to hide pages removed from her son's books within the folds of her sari. Rassundari wrote her autobiography in two parts, the earlier part which was written in the late 1870s gives a more comprehensive account of her life. She felt strongly about being denied education, and reflected, "women were indeed unfortunate, and could be counted as being like animals". But "my mind would not accept this, and it was always restless with the urge to learn"[14].

In the early years it was not unusual for illiterate or semiliterate women to talk about their lives to scribes; these were published sometimes several decades later. After the middle of the last century, when newspapers, journals and public meetings discussed women's education, spoke for or against child marriage, widow re-marriage and the system of *purdah* or female seclusion, women from *bhadralok* families started writing about their lives as well as commenting on the above issues. In addition, the role of the *bhadramahila* in changing Bengali society, relations with her husband and the need for greater awareness on health, hygiene and child-care were discussed in the growing number of women's journals and magazines.[15] Koilashbashini Debi's *Jonoika Grihabadhur Diary* (A Certain Housewife's Diary)[16] is in the form of reminiscences of her life between 1846 and 1875 and was put together and published only in 1953. It would appear that she kept rough notes which she organised only after her husband's death in 1873, when she was 44 years old. As experiences of almost forty years are compressed in a little over thirty printed pages, clearly she wrote selectively on issues which she remembered well and had been influenced by. An important theme in Koilashbashini's writings is her evolving relationship with her husband, Kissory Chand Mitra, whom she married when she was 11, and the tensions his reformist tendencies created in her mind. Kissory Chand and his brother Peary Chand were both deeply influenced by the ideology of the Brahmo reform movement as well as by Derozio's Young Bengal Group. They reacted against polygamy and believed firmly that women should be educated. Accordingly, Kissory Chand taught his wife himself and later arranged for an English woman tutor for her. He was a man of letters, being the editor of the *Indian Field* and a regular contributor to the *Calcutta Review*. While it is not clear whether he actually joined the Brahma Samaj, he was greatly impressed by many of its tenets and had several friends who were its members. Like many young men of his time, he become excessively addicted to liquor, and his premature death was attributed to interference in food and drink[17].

Though Koilashbashini did not mention how her husband died, the last few pages of her diary reflected a certain helpless sorrow. She menioned more than once her reservations about the company that he had started keeping on their return to Calcutta after a happy life in the districts. The fact that Koilashbashini wrote as freely as she did on her friendship with her husband as well as about her anguish over his last few years is indicative of a degree of candour not expected of a Hindu widow. But then, Kissory Chand Mitra's wife had been exposed to much more than most average middle class Bengali women. In addition, through education she had a acquired the ability to express herself freely : her *Diary* was her confidante in later life. She was also, in many ways, a fitting example of a *Zenana* educated women. A certain degree of fluency in both English and Bengali meant that she was able to read fairly extensively as well as liken her lonely *mofussil* (district) life to that of Robinson Crusoe's. She was also able to teach her young daughter, Kumudini. Unlike other educated women of her day, Koilashbashini decided to write about her life. Though we are given no reason for her wanting to do so her *Diary* clearly fufiilled an important note in her later life : through its pages she freely expressed the dilemmas faced by a women caught between tradition and the inexorable forces of changes during those action-packed years.

In many ways, Koilashbashini's conflicts reflected, in microcosm, the drama being enacted on a much bigger stage. When, in around the 1830s, Kissory Chand Mitra was first attracted to the reform movement, it was entering its most dynamic phase; by the time he died, the movement was deeply divided. one of the major issues of debate being the role of women and how they should be equipped to face change. Not unexpectedly. the nature and extent of women's education was an important talking point. While the more orthodox, and certainly dominant sections of Hindu society were unwilling to educate their womenfolk at all, Brahmos too were not united on this question. For most. the ideal was *Zenana* education which conveniently combined the notion of feminine seclusion with a modicum of basis learning However, the demand for girls schooling was fast gaining ground, and in 1849, the first *bhadralok* attempts in this area attained fruition : the Calcutta Female School (later known as the Bethune School) was established largely due to the fund-raising efforts of a number of men committed to educating their daughters[18]. Governmental support was ensured through the active collaboration of J.E.D. Bethune, legal member of the Governor-General's Council and later President of the Council of Education. Bethune was convinced that the *bhadralok* would sooner rather than later "feel the want of companions, the cultivations of whose taste and intellect might correspond in some degree to his own"[19]. He was not wrong as the Western educated Salariat were indeed looking for the ideal helpmate, educated and reasonably enlightened. However, it was not until the closing phase of the century that prejudices against schooling for girls were gradually worn down.

Between the years 1863 and 1890, the number of girl's schools went up from 95 to 2238 and the number of school-going girls from 2,486 to 78,865[20]. The majority were primary school students. Clearly, a certain amount of deliberation in many homes lay behind this expansion. By and large, opinion on the education of girls was divided along the following lines ; While Dwarakanath Ganguly, Sivanath Sastri and other radical Brahmos felt that as both men and women should have equal chances in life, there was no justification for the study of separate subjects or limits to the level to which girls should be educated, mainstream Brahmos led by Keshub Chander Sen and Umesh Chandra Datta, editor of the influential *Bamabodhini Patrika* (Journal for the Enlightenment of women) as well as a section of more enlightened Hindus were advocates of limited education for girls, with a separate curriculum. On the other hand, conservative Hindus, most of whom were not prepared to go beyond a modicum of *Zenana* education, were greatly concerned with the harmful effects of education, which they felt would make women negligent of their families and lax in house keeping. In the early 1860s, the *Bamabodhini Patrika* (which was founded by the followers of Sen) had started a scheme of education for girls and women through correspondence, known as *antahpur shiksha* (home education). As a feasible alternative to a few years of schooling in a formal institution this course provided the opportunity for girls to continue with learning even after they were married.[21]

Zenana education through the columns of the *Bamabodhini Patrika* as well as from home tutors continued to be the most popular form and method of education for girls for several years. Koilashbashini's reflections on life were clearly influenced by contemporary events as well as by all that she had been through personally. For her, reform had been a bitter-sweet experience : on the one had while it had meant personal emancipation and the evolution of a meaningful martial relationship, it had on the other, also involved putting up with a style of life which ultimately spelt destruction for her immediate family. Koilashbashini who was 11 years old when she was married, had a great eye for detail, dates and names : the description of each incident or occasion was accompanied by meticulous information of the day, month and year as well as of the persons encountered. Her ability to enjoy the countryside and the experience of travelling for days on end along the waterways of East Bengal are evocatively described. Her visit to Plassey—"where the British and the nawabs first fought"—was an exciting event : she wrote "even though at that time I felt the loss of my son acutely, I experienced a deep sense of satisfaction when I came home". After the birth of her daughter in 1847 she wrote : "My mother-in-law was very sad. She said, "I have lost gold and got glass instead". Koilashbashini did not dwell on her mother-in-law's feelings much but goes on to describe Kissory Chand's responses, and the discomforts of her confinement. Her husband wrote to say that he was very happy and that "you should feel no sorrow. All are the same in the eyes of the *Jagatpita* (father of the word, or God). We should also treat all equally. I am awaiting the time when you will be able to write to me"[22]. But it was a long time before Koilashbashini could reply, confined as she was to a room which she linkened to a "kind of jail room". For over a month, the upper caste post-partum woman was not to touch anything nor communicate with others except functionaries assigned specific tasks.

She wrote—

> "But my husband did not know my situation. In every letter he wrote, "you are so cruel, you are so heartless; I did't know that you'd be so happy at my suffering. In every letter I ask you to write one line but you don't write. I won't write to you any more". I was greatly concerned; if he did not write for two or three days, I would die"[23].

Soon, the determined Koilashbashini found pen and paper to write to her lonely husband.

With their young daughter Kumudini, the couple soon started touring the mofussil areas together, often spending long days on the river "when we played cards an chatted." Koilashbashini kept track of her husband's work and proudly reported the establishment of a hospital or a school. Wherever possible, she made friends with other Bengali women. About her life in Natore, (Where she was fortunate in having a number of women to befriend). She says "we were happy. The reason for this was that as women our demands were few, our minds slight; hence, we were satisfied with little; that independence was enough". Obviously, Koilashbashini was referring to the freedom to interact with other women and occasionally bathe with them in the river at dawn.

> "When Babu (her husband) went out in the sun or to the mofussil areas, those days all of us used to wander in the garden. There was no restriction on that. You (referring to her husband) also used to walk with me in the garden, but then they (her women friends) could not join : they did not come out before my husband, nor did I appear before their husbands[24]".

Nonetheless, for Koilashbashini the world of purdah has its consolations : once when she was ill, and her female attendant was not available, her husband took care of all her needs. While family members used to visit the districts occasionally, the young couple spent most of the time on their own. On her visits to either her parents or her in-laws, Koilashbashini recounted how she used to be counting the days for her return to her husband. Kissory Chand used to teach her English, and in 1852 when he was posted to Calcutta, he engaged an English women, Miss Tugod, as tutor for his wife. This lady used to teach two other *bhadramahilas* also, and was paid Rs. 25 by each family. Koilashbashini added "and there was tuition from the home *quru* (her husband) as well. In this way a certain amount of knowledge was acquired[25]". In Jahanabad there were not many women whom Koilashbashini could befriend :

> "My daughter and my husband were my only support. I did not see the faces of any other living

being. Not that this caused me much discomfort. When he used to go to the mofussil, I used to live like Robinson Crusoe. I ate, slept, read and did needle-work. I also taught my daughter and wrote this book. And I used to count the days for his return. When my husband came back, I was greatly relieved[26]".

Life changed for Koilashbashini when her husband became a junior Magistrate in Calcutta; the last few pages of her brief Diary make frequent mention of her husband's growing attraction for the more Westernised, liberal Bengalis, many of whom were Brahmos. Kissory Chand obviously enjoyed the ideas of his new friends, where no doubt discussions were carried out over a glass of port or wine. When Koilashbashini objected, her husband chided her affectionately, but did not give much attention to her protestations. As her husband's interaction with social reformers increased, Koilashbashini too started mixing with their wives. At the homes of eminent Brahmos Ramtanu Lahiri and Ramgopal Ghosh, she ate food prepared by a cook and served by a Muslim bearer. Though she clearly found the situation some what unusual, strong conviction of the validity of her own way of life left her unaffected. She reported,

> "I told Babu about Ramtanu Babu's wife. Babu asked "Where did she eat"? I replied, "why, with everyone else. After all who am I or who is she, or who is anyone for that matter"? Babu replied" that indeed is true and it is only Bengalis who make an unnecessary fuss". I don't believe in Hindu rituals, but nonetheless I observe them. The reason for this is that if I slacken even a bit, my husband, will cease being a Hindu. The Hindus are my closest relatives. I cannot give them up and hence I observe all the rituals...My husband can do what he likes, there is no problem in that. Bengalis observe this religion, and hence those who have brains, do not observe the Bengali religion. I don't believe in

> it but I will never tell my husband this. If Babu heard this from my lips I cannot describe how happy he would be[27]".

While Koilashbashini was not actively hostile to the Brahmo faith, she was reluctant to give up what she had been brought up to believe in. In a particularly dramatic passage she described her discussion with Kissory Chand regarding their differing beliefs. She told her husband that as from Childhood he had been teaching her as one would teach a pet bird to speak, "I cannot have any views that are basically different from yours. But I will not leave Hinduism and I have given you the reasons Thy". Her husband retorted "Do you have so little belief in me"? To which Koilashbashini replied, "No that can never be; but I do not believe in your style of life." Finally, "Babu understood and did not say anything more[28]". Koilashbashini's questioning and sceptical mind was critical of both the social reform movement as well as of Hinduism. However, on balance she felt that it was more expeditious to uphold certain Hindu values at a time when families were being torn apart by religious and social dissenssions.

The year that the Company Rule ended "there was a comet sighted in the sky and in the month of *as win*, there was a terrible earthquake". It also brought to an end, Kissory Chand's employment with the British and he was unceremoniously stripped of his title of Rai Bahadur. In the days that followed, Koilashbashini consoled him and even suggested that she could contribute to the family income by selling her needlework. Her husband was apparently appreciative of her support and understanding :

> "Babu said" I have gained great courage from your words...From your words I realise that you are as brave as I am, that you are as intelligent as I am and in fact that your staying power is greater than mine. In knowing this all my pain has gone[29]".

The pages Koilashbashini's *Diary* are alive with descriptions of her relationship with her husband, which among other things was characterised by a strong sense of companionship and mutual respect. They not only played cards with each other, read together but also argued on matters of considerable social and religious significance. Koilashbashini's writings give the distinct impression that not only were the discussions frank and forthright, but also that Kissory Chand often accepted his wife's point of view and reasoning. Despite her maintenance of strict *purdah*, travels in the districts of Bengal gave Koilashbashini insights into different ways of life. The fact that Kissory Chand has chosen to keep his wife and child with him provided for the development of a strong family bond where both partners looked upon the home as a refuge from the fast changing world outside. Judging by the narration of events, neither Koilashbashini's family nor that of her conjugal home had much of a role to play in their lives. Though as a dutiful daughter-in-law she attended every important family function, Koilashbashini never failed to recount how both she and her husband were counting the days for her return.

Jonoika Grihabadur Diary is remarkable for its candour and insights. It describes in some detail the life of an Indian working for the East India Company through the eyes of a woman who was educated enough not only to teach her child, be familiar with the scriptures of other religious but also to write lucidly on moral and social issues. At the end of the *Diary*, the editors have included a page of monthly accounts and details of jewellery, both of which were meticulously maintained by Koilashbashini. Without the all encompassing purview of older family members and in-laws Koilashbashini developed a strong sense of personal identity and was quite clear, particularly in the early years of her marriage, on her role in preserving domestic harmony : though she did make occasional statements about the limitations of a woman's mind, her well-reasoned response to Hinduism at the level of ritual and behaviour convey the impression of a balanced, independent-minded woman.

Koilashbashini's Diary starts in the year her sou died and ends with the death of Kissory Chand in 1873 :

> "Oh reader, here my book ends. Today my life is finished...I came back a widow. When this name (widow) comes to my ears, it is like a thunderbolt. Alas, what a frightening name (word) – hearing it is like having a heart attack[30]" :

It is possible that Koilashbashini's apprehensions of widowhood were based on an awareness of the singularly oppressive and limited life of a Hindu widow. What is more possible, however, is that her agonised words lamented the premature end of a life of companionship and mutual trust. This evolution of a husband-wife bond with limited interference from the larger family collectivity was not usual in Nineteenth Century Bengal. To characterise it as a marriage based on the 'romantic love' notion which was growing in the west would also perhaps be inappropriate. It would be more realistic to Koilashbashini's attitude to Kissory Chand as being one of *bhakti* or devotion, of thanks-giving to a man she admired. and who had done much for her. But her account is not free from a certain implicit regret and a feeling that after a point of time, situations had overtaken her. While she did not express openly her resentment at this turn of events, it is implied in many of her musings. Koilashbashini was a combination of an independent minded woman, who nonetheless knew when and how to give in. She was a fine strategist who combined tact with a degree of firmness. Yet, in the ultimate analysis, she was a helpless and lonely figure in a world where men and the male way of life determined the fate of families.

Despite the fact that Koilashbashini was unable to control her husband's excessive addiction to food and drink, her well-argued stand against certain aspects of Hinduism as well as of the social reform movement clearly prove that women of the *antahpur* were well-trained in the art of survival and manoeuvre. Far from being the archetypal model "underground self" to be condemned, if not rescued, from all-pervading ignorance, the *antahpur* was a well-ordered, hierarchical realm with functions divided amongst its members. Like the world outside, the *antahpur* was governed by certain specific rules on interaction and roles, determined and judged by women within the framework of a male-dominated society. Though a primary function was providing essential resources to the menfolk, women managed to develop sufficient physical and psychological space for themselves within the confines of their living quarters.[31]

Written from the point of view of one deeply affected by social change, Koilashbashini's *Diary* provides insights into how an individual women responded to the events influencing her life : her story is neither a paean for change, nor an indictment of it. Rather, it provides a realistic assessment of how she was affected and influenced. Using the tools of literacy provided to her by these very forces of change, Koilashbashini gives us a fairly vivid idea of her life and its concomitant tensions. She started reading and writing in her mid-teens by which time she had been socialised into the ethos of the *antahpur*; nonetheless, she looked eagerly to the male preserve of learning, combining her innate commitment to order and continuity with her desire for access to the new knowledge. Her education gave her the skill to express herself on paper : learning did not merely create an unthinkingly devoted helpmate but also a questioning, and at times a troubled mind. The *Diary* is, in many senses, the story of a woman, who, like Virginia Wolf was painfully aware of the angel hovering around her. In part, her apprehensions regarding the social reform movement indicated Koilashbashini's willingness to question some of the values of the Western-oriented yet staunchly male-dominated society. Ultimately, her tenacity in sticking by tradition was of little use as she became a helpless witness to her husband's self-destruction. As a woman, she was in no position to impose her will on his : though she had in some areas resisted Kissory Chand's dominance; she was, by and large, his creation, his willing student. Nor did Koilashbashini write openly on her ultimate anguish, of her suffering as her life's companion abandoned an existence of simple pleasures for the more compelling intellectual stimulation and way of life of his peers.

Education did not result in too many Koilashbashinis; what it did so, however, was to provide the basis for fundamental change in women's lives. It gave those who were interested, access to new kinds of information as well as to a certain way of thinking and analysing situations. Though only a handful of women (as also men) perhaps had the time and inclination to reflect on their position in a changing environment, even a randon sampling of autobiographical writings indicates that *antahpur* women did not live in a state of benighted ignorance, nor did they unquestioningly take to the changes being introduced. Life in the *antahpur* was orderly, well-organised and goal-or-iented. When education was introduced as an additional input if not as a counter point to the values of this life-most women took to it readily. At the same time, they had to combine learning with an already full day of house-work. In addition, many felt, like Koilashbashini, that there was a stake in keeping traditional values intact. Here, women mediated and decided what education was to mean to them; not all were *tabula rasas* to be worked upon by crusading reformers commited to redemption. Social change is after all basically a process of interaction of mutual give and take. So far, we have only had the evidence of those individuals and institutions who are popularly known as the agents of change. To get a more unbiased picture of reality it is essential to know more about those whose lives were the target of these changes. The reading of *Jonoika Grihabahadur Diary* is an attempt in this process of getting more information about what actually went on within homes and how the hitherto invisible were affected in those turbulent years of nineteenth century Bengal.

REFERENCES

1. Joan Wallach Scott puts forth this view in her "New Documents on the Lives of French Women : The Journal of Caroline B, 1864-1868". p. 568 of *Signs*, Vol. 12, No. 3 1987.

2. Neera Desai *et. al* discuss this view of women's studies in their "Women's Studies and Social Sciences in India", UNESCO, mimeo. 1982.

3. Over here I have used the term 'middle class' to include mainly the newly emergent white collar salariat as well as some sections of the landed gentry who had moved to the urban areas in search of alternate forms of employment.

4. Said, Edward; *Orientalism*, London : Routledge and Kegan Paul, 1978, p. 3.

5. Michael Allen discussses some prevailing notions of Indian feminity in his "The Hindu view of Women" in M. Allen and S N. Mukherjee's edited *Women in India and Nepal*; Canberra, Australian National University Monographs on South-Asia No 8, 1982. In her "The Mythological Film, and its Framework of Meaning: Analysis of Jai Santoshi Ma", (*India International Centre Quarterly*, March 1980) Veena Das looks at the runaway film hit and analyses the *Sati* image as well as that of female shakti. The basis for a women's power is her role in reproduction; hence the consequent stress on the maintenance of purity of the lineage by controlling women and their sexual powers. In this context, see Leela Dube's "Seed and Earth : the Symbolision of Biological Reproduction and Sexual Relations of Production" in Leela Dube *at al's* edited *Visibility and Power-Essays on Women in Society and Development*, New Delhi Oxford University Press, 1986.

6. See J H. Broomfield's *Elite Conflict in a Plural Society* Bombay : Oxford University Press, 1968. p. 13 onwards for a discussion of the term *bhadralok*. While Broomfield envisaged the *bhadralok* as a distinct category, Rajat Kanta Ray in his *Social Conflict and Political Unrest in Bengal 1875-1927* New Delhi : Oxford University Press, 1984, is more inclined to conceptualise the *bhadralok* as comprising "respectable society" rather than a homogenous group

7. To date, four volumes of essays entitled *Subaltern Studies* have been published. This quotation is from page 1 of Ranajit Guha's "On Some Aspects of the Historiography of Colonial India" in *Subaltern Studies I*, New Delhi, Oxford University Press, 1982.

8. The Bangladeshi historians Ghulam Murshid's most informative *Reluctant Debutante : Response of Bengali Women to Modernisation 1849-1905* (Rajshahi University Press,. *1982*), and Meredith Borthwick's *The Changing Role of Women in Bengal 1849-1985* (Princeton: Princeton University Press, 1984) provide considerable material on attitudes to and of women during this period. Borthwick categorises the *bhadramahilas* as the women from *bhadralok* homes and deals at

length with their responses to education, the family, marriage and so on. In Bengali, Chtira Deb's *Antahpurer Atmakatha* (*The Autobiography of the home*), Calcutta Ananda publications, 1984, gives a comprehensive account of women's responses to home life based on quotations and descriptions from various autobiographies written by women. In addition, "*Daimalir Karagar Bhangar Gaan*" (*Daimali's Song of Prison Destruction* by Srabashi Gosh published in the *Sharadiya Anushtup* 1985 analyses some trends in Bengali women's autobiographies. See also her "*Birds in a Cage*", Changes in Bengali Social Life as Recorded sn Autobiographies by Women" in the *Economic and Political Weekly, issue on Women Studies*, October 25, 1986, Vol. XXI, No. 43.

9. Gilbert, Sandra, and Susan Gubar, *The Madwomen in the Attic*, New Haven, Yale University Press, 1979.

10. *Ibid*, p. 6.

11. *Ibid*, p. 8.

12 The notion of the angel in the house is described so well by Virginia Wolfe in the essay "Professions for Women", included in her Volume *The Death of the Moth*, (London : Hogarth Press, 194[illegible]) pp. 149-153 This quotation is from p. 150 of Wolfes brilliant characterisation of the dilemma of the women author.

13. Sharadusundari Devi dictated her life to her grandson-in-law Jogendralal Khastigir. It was published in Bengali as *Atmakantha* (Autobiography) in 1913.

14. From p.28 of Rassundari's *Amar Jiban* included in Vol. 1 of NareshChandra Jana *et, al's Atmakatha*, Calcutta; Ananya Prakashan, 1981.

15. See Borthwick, Chapters Three and Eight.

16. Kailashbashini Debi's *Jonoika Grihbadhur Diary* was serialised in the Bengali monthly, *Basumati* in 1953 and has recently been put together in the Bengali Literary and Cultural Journal, *Akkhon* special issue of 1982, pp. 9-48. Present references are from this version, and I have done the translation.

17. While there is no biography of Kissory Chand, I have gleaned these details on his life from various sources as well as appendix II, pp. 170-1 of Roper Leth bridge *A History of the Renaissance in Bengal, Ramtonu Lahiri : Brahman and Reformer*, Calcutta, Indian Edition 1982 (first published in 1907).

18. See J.C. Bagal's *Women's Education in Eastern India*, Calcutta : The World Press Private Ltd., 1956 Ch. VII, "The Bethune School" for a description of the establishment of the school and also his es say

entitled "History of the Bethune School and College" in the *Bethune School* and College Centenary Volume, Calcutta, N.D.

19. Quoted from p. 1C9 of Bagal *Op, cit.*

20. From Murshid, page 43. Murshid discusses this attitude in Chapter I of the *Reluctant Debutante*, See also Borthwick, Chapter One for a description of emerging feminine roles.

21. In Appendix two, Murshid describes *Zenana* education in full. While a number of journals for women had started appearing by this time, *Bamobodhini Patrika and Tattvabodhini Patrika*, and later Dwarakanath Ganguly's *Abalabandhab* were the most important journals for women. Earlier in Chapter I, he discusses attitudes to women's education. See also Borthwick, Chapter I.
Koilashbashini Debi, *Op. cit.*, p. 10.

23. *Ibid.*, p. 11.

24. *Ibid.*, p. 18

25. *Ibid* , p. 30.

26. *Ibid.*, p. 21.

27. *Ibid* . p. 32.

28. Ibid., pp. 32. From page 31 onwards, Koliashbashini starts discussing in some detail the dilemma facing her.

29. *Ibid.*, p. 14-35.

30. *Ibid.*, p. 41.

31. Based on my readings of autobiographies and other sources I have dealt with life in the *antahpur* in my on-going project entitled, "Changing Family Strategies and Educated Women : A case Study from Bengal". See also Deb and Borthwick for details on *antahpur* life.

CHAPTER FOUR

Use of Field-Work in Research on Women

DR. PRABHA MAHALE

In this paper I have tried to bring out the importance of conducting field-work or participatory research in getting to know women's real life experiences and perceptions, past and present. Drawing from my own experience of an ongoing research project on "Women's Work and Family Strategies : A study of Basavis in Karnataka" I also deal with three questions 1) How I planned the field-work for this project ? (2) How I formulated my research question and 3) what technique and sources did I use in the research. Issues related with women, their rights, role and status for the most part have remained either invisible or have received no attention of the academic community. Thus, our understanding of the social reality is very much distorted as information about women who constitute almost half the humanity has been left out from all academic pursuits. Dale Spender's statement (quoted by Prof. Neera Desai) provides us a better insight into this lack of information. To quote, "Research which is addressed to the problems of the production of knowledge in a systematic fashion, is a relatively recent phenomenon. Analysing the power base and power relations which are inherent in the codification of knowledge *is still understandably* not always viewed as a laudable or legitimate activity. But in recent years there has been a shift towards the recognition that knowledge is socially constructed, that it is invented by human beings with limited access to explanations and limited claims to infallibility......Most of the knowledge produced in our society has been produced by men, they have usually generated the explanations and the schemata and have then checked with each other and vouched for the accuracy and adequacy of their view of the world...women have been excluded as the producers of knowledge and as the subjects of knowledge for men have often made their own knowledge and their own sex representative of humanity". Women's Studies challenge the very premisses of the existing knowledge and seek to construct new knowledge. And in order to render invisible women visible and to obtain a better insight and understanding of the position of women in its historical and contemporary contents a reappraisal of existing methodology is as much necessary as a programme of research on women. This seminar is a unique attempt to bring together researchers from different disciplines to share their research experiences.

Let us review the contribution of two disciplines, to our understanding of women, namely, History and Anthropology that deal with the past and present human life respectively. For too long now, historians have been prone to treat women, as also many other social scientists as invisible. Thus, best of our historians have been victims of blindness towards women and their contribution to social system. In order to put the record straight and tackle the problem of the myth about women's invisibility, a major task for scholars in Women's Studies will be to unearth the hidden history from the perspective of women, which necessitates an understanding of historical development and simultaneously a thorough probe of women's role in it. Without an adequate understanding of the historical dimension of women's situation it would be difficult to develop any new theoretical perspective. Also to make a realistic assessment of the position of women in their present social set up an important aspect of our research will have to be addressed to the depiction of women implicit or explicit in history.

Anthropology, the science of man and his works that claims to be covering the entire range of human experiences and interactions has fared no better than the other social sciences in reflecting the diversities that characterize women's lives, their roles, values and concerns. In fact the anthropologists are better equipped to uncover the reality of women's life and their contribution to the social system with their methods of field research and subject matter that considers a study of the reality of the people's life, their culture as a legitimate sphere of their investigation. Yet the main stream anthropology in writing about human culture has paid greater attention to the masculine activities and interests and women and their issues have always been considered secondary : if not peripheral to the understanding of society and culture. This often is attributed to the male-bias. Another reason for the misrepresentation of the reality of women's lives and their contribution to social life is due to the fact that most anthropologists have been males who as a result of their maleness had little or no access to women in the field. Male researchers often relay on male informants and observe activities of males or those involving both sexes but rarely those in which women alone participate. Thus, though in anthropology a great deal of information about women exists, it frequently comes from questions asked of men about their wives, daughters and sisters. rather than from women themselves. Thus, we get a distorted picture of the women's life.

To me the histortan wanting to write women's history in the absence of any recorded history of women is placed in the same situation as the anthropologist who is interested in studying the non-literate tribal communities. In the absence of written records or studies the anthropologist does not find his/her documents ready-made. But makes them "by direct experience of living or by interview and record". Through empirical or first hand field research one draws primary data from life itself-from the actions, words and even gestures of the people among whom one lives and with the help of oral tradition, the anthropologist tends to write the history of his/her subjects as it were backwards. The time-tested methodology of field-research developed by the anthropologist proves immensely useful in understanding the reality of women's lives. When I say this I do not disregard or under estimate the value of other methods.

Thus, in order to make available to the society women's contribution and perspective past and present, we will have to construct the knowledge about the lives of women and for this we will have to make use of multiple sources of data. In the absence of historical documents depicting the contributions of women, more urgent attention needs to be paid to the great treasure of history remaining in the memories of the women who lived through these times. Thus women themselves are to be considered the major source of information about women and unless we soon conduct field research with persons within living memories of the past this knowledge will be irretrievably lost.

A people's oral tradition or oral history is important for the further reason that it forms a part of the thought of the living population and hence a part of their social life which we can directly observe. In other words, the history of the past is incapsulated in a context of present thought and thus belongs to the present and through field study it can be captured to some extent. This brings me to the use of field work in creating new knowledge on women.

While exclusive attention to women in our research is likely to lead to another kind of distortion and will not give a proper understanding of the social reality, it is as much necessary to consider them as social actors and to know their point of view and their activities as it is of men. Women who are as much a part of a culture as the men are, if are not understood properly neither are men. Because the roles of men and women in a society are so intricately interwoven that a partial understanding of one sex would of necessity involve a distorted understanding of the other. So what we need in general is a new approach, one that would concentrate on the world view, beliefs and activities of both men and women and on their inter-relationships in any given cultural system. Thus to have a balanced picture of the social reality while conducting field research it is always advisable to have a pair of researchers of both sexes. Particularly in collecting women's life histories, same gender interviewing is highly preferable because women informants are certainly going to feel more comfortable in an interview interaction with a female researcher.

Further, whether the researchers are male or female they should necessarily have sensitivity to women's concern. This I am saying from my own experience. Because though I had specialized in the field of education and enculturation and had come accross wide variations in the percentage of male-female literacy, their rate of drop-outs and different role models for boys and girls in their enculturation, neither did I heed much attention to the casual factors of these variations, nor did I consider women as a special category for investigation. The facts were accepted as given in the social context without reasoning. I must confess that towards the end of 1983 I had the good fortune to attend and participate in the U.G.C. sponsored workshop organized by research Unit on Women's Studies of S.N.D.T. Women's University, Bombay for orientation of teachers in Women's Studies and it was here for the first time that I was sensitized to the women's question.

More or less at the same time there was extensive reporting in the news papers about the wide-spread prevalence of the Basavi practice in Karnataka. The practice refers to sanctified harlotory, wherein women and girls of scheduled castes like Madar, Holeya and Bedas, the Scheduled tribe community are dedicated to deities, idols, objects of worship whereby the consecrated women are barred from marriage and are obliged by custom to prostitute themselves, Inspite of legal measures like SITA 1956 and Devadasi Prohibition Act (1981), the practice continues undeterred in some parts of the state. The newspaper reporting was that over five thousand women are dedicated every year at Savdatti and a major portion of them are transported to the red light areas of Bombay and Pune.

A review of the existing literature on Basavi practice showed that except for the two studies of Punekar and Kamala Rao and Harshad Trivedi that dealt with the socio-economic background of these women there was no other detailed in-depth study available about these women. In order to locate and analyse factors and processes that could explain the condition of these women and to understand the forces that lead to the violation of legal provisions, I felt a need for an empirical field-study of the life situations of these Basavis, their self-perceptions and their status within the family and society.

A preliminary investigation about the practice pointed out that the girls or women thus dedicated were invested with masculine previleges such as those normally enjoyed by the son, like, they continued the patrilineal line of the parents, performed their funeral rites and inherited their property. In a society where there is no system which is absolutely egalitarian or non-discriminative to women, the fact that a Basavi thus is endowed with masculine privileges and no stigma is attached to her or her children and that she enjoys higher status than other women of her caste needed to be examined. I did not start my research with a well formulated problem, a properly enunciated initial hypothesis or a well drawn-out research design, as, these are not considered a must for anthropological research and their absence is in line with the method of ethnographic investigation. Anthropological practice is against sharp definitions in terms of the investigator's perspective and actual first-hand research decides what is to be done and what is not to be done. However, the absence of a very well-defined and delimited problem of research does not mean that the research was started in a vacuum. I did decide about the broad areas of investigation concerning the institution of Basavi and identified four major areas of the life of Basavis for investigation in the field, which were to be revised, added to or changed according to the need in the particular field.

The first area of enquiry, I considered important was the family household composition-the concrete context within which normally a family is expected or assumed to function is absent in this social situation as the biological and social father of the children is absent in most cases and it was felt necessary to understand how these female headed households operate and the kind of rights, duties and obligations the women and men have in these family units, their descent and inheritance pattern.

The second area that interested me was the social and cultural context and the underlying economic implications of the practice. Here the important questions that the study addresses are,—to what extent the caste and classs background act as important determinants of the Basavi System, are women used as objects of social mobility by their families, what special status and privileges do the Basavis enjoy in the family, community and in the society as a whole ? It was also significant to understand the basis of the system in terms of the religious sanctions, myths, the popular legends, the ritual of branding, deflowering ceremony etc.

The third area is the organization of work and the family strategies-work which is open to the dedicated daughter namely prostitution or concubinage is not open to a married woman and hence what is the contribution that a woman makes through it to the family survival, maintenance and reproduction needed investigation. Further what other work these women are engaged in ? How are the family strategies evolved? Are the decisions to dedicate a girl made within or outside the family and if outside the family, what are these out of family forces ?

The fourth area deals with querries about the self-perception of the Basavis and those of others in the society-Do the

Basavis perceive themselves as objects of exploitation by their families, or the rest of the society ? How do they compare themselves with married women of their community, what is their status compared to other women and men in the community, what role do these Basavis play in perpetuating the practice ? What are the perceptions of their parents, children community members and other castes ?

In focussing on these areas of investigation my objective was to have a clearer understanding of the Basavi practice, how it operates and affects the lives of women in terms of their social-cultural context. While enumerating this long list of questions that I sought to research in the field what I want to draw to your attention is that while focussing our attention on a specific women's issue we will have to have a multi-dimensional approach and a critical mind to question the basis of the present in egalitarian system. Further we need to begin the field research with the assumption that a people's life is a totality in which every aspect is interconnected with the other and this interlinkage is to be found by seeing the various aspects of life in actual operation. In brief, the first hand field-work or empirical research is to be carried out with a holistic perspective and we must plunge into the fieldwork with an open mind to understand how the people (women) actually live. For this we have to employ a fully participant approach in research. Some of the techniques adopted while conducting field research and the details of topical coverage are.

Only as a researcher lives her/his way into a system of customs overtime can she know and so be able to report explicitly. a total context of behaviour. So, long term residence ranging from one to one and a half years in the midst of the subjects of study and total immersion in their culture is an essential part of the field-work. The techniques of participant-observation and interviewing are the mainstays of field-research. The field-worker must examine precise details of behaviour in a number of action settings. For, failure to employ a fully participant approach in women's research may block out important aspects of women's experience. Hence, while making the choice of the living quarters one should select a house that is centrally located in the field of study. This enables one to see events of daily life as they happen. Participant observation as a technique of data gathering assumes great significance in field studies on women. Because women when questioned often make statements about ideal norms of behaviour or give information which fits into the roles models generally accepted by the society at large, though the actual reality could be something else. The significant discrepancies between what women say they do and what they actually do can be checked through observation. Keeping a daily diary and nothing every detail of one's observations about the actions of women is necessary-these women then appear as actors in a series of different circumstances who manipulate choices of norms to suit the requirement of particular situation. While participating to the extent possible the researcher, on the basis of watching the ongoing behaviour, can collect observational data on daily work, rituals, the working of caste councils, initiation ceremonies, festivals etc. In rituals events like marriage, funerals etc., the positioning of persons in the scene practically always reflects important social information which is difficult to obtain through interview techniques.

As I have already pointed out, in the field-work primary data is drawn from life itself from the actions, words and even gestures of the people among whom one lives. Because of this, field-work becomes essentially a collaborative enterprise, an interaction between the field worker and the subjects of his study and winning the confidence of the people becomes an absolute necessity to collect reliable data. To gain the confidence of the subjects, each field-worker has to make efforts to establish a good rapport with the people. It is only by extended familiarity with the subjects that one can overcome their initial distrust. The personal bond that I have established with my life history subjects has made them to confide in me and freely share their personal agonies of life and happiness-the women spoke for themselves, about their activities and work and their concerns of life.

Conducting an initial survey of households through a census schedule served many purposes. First, it helped to establish contact with the community. Second, it provided me with quantified data on social-cultural and demographic details of the population i.e. it gave a basis for placing my study into a context. Third, it helped in selecting key informants or subjects of life history. The data collected for each household includes data on all the members of the household, their names, their place of birth, age, marital and educational status, occupation, relation to the household head, clan affiliation of the household and ownership family income, ownership of material goods, details of dedications in the family, the family deity etc.

The meaning and functioning of the behaviour, customs, rituals observed can be obtained through informal, indepth unscripted interviewing, talk and discussion either singly or in groups. Also, information regarding those behaviours that cannot be observed directly also can be obtained through interviewing. If for e.g. during the field-work no one has died, then, to understand the funeral rites, one has to depend on interview technique. Again we do not use any questionnaire or interview schedule but have a topical guide which is used only to sensitize the interviewer to areas of investigation. Interview data may be distorted and hence the accuracy can be gained through cross checking the data from different informants and also through repeating the same questions in a variety of interview settings over a period of time.

Oral traditions like a whole lot of songs, folktales, myths, as well as data on religious beliefs and practices related to the Basavi practice is also collected for content analysis. Genealogies which link living people with their dead ancestors and to others around them are used as an analytical tool to study the kinship system. Genealogies have helped to understand the relationships by descent, and marriage. Conditions in one generation when contrasted and compared with those in other, provide some indication of the extent of dedication and change in the pattern if any. Through the genealogies, I find that among the Bedas they had a practice of dedicating every girl born in the family and the wives were brought from outside. Data on Life cycle ritulas and ancestor worship too is collected to understand the difference in the status of women of different categories and the man.

While dealing with illiterate subjects there is no question of availability of written accounts and biographies because they themselves could not write diaries and who would write their biography as they were the common and not distinguished personalities.

Life history narratives or focused biographies of the dedicated women are collected for they provide resource material for understanding life experiences at different points in their life cycle in specific cultural and historical setting. A life history is a type of oral history embodying the story of a woman's life constructed from her oral account, that provides invaluable access to the experiences and perceptions and emotional realities of women whose lives otherwise simply are inaccessible to us today. We ask women to speak for and about themselves-about their own work and their own lives rather than about history. We want to know about the private lives, about their emotions. But why should they tell us and relieve sometimes painful memories with almost a total stranger. Only by winning the confidence and convincing a person that their lives have historical meaning, we can do a life history. While selecting subjects for life history interviewing, the factors of caste, class and age were considered to cover the variegated spectrum of social life. Also the women who are willing to share parts of their lives with us are to be selected.

Collecting life histories meant doing two things. First, I worked with the woman whom I interviewed to discover and explore her life and second I posed questions seeking clarification and content. In a life-history interviewing it is necessary that we do not use a structured interview guide but leave it to the women to speak for and about themselves on any aspect of life that is of great concern to them. This, to me, cannot be done just in one sitting. The researcher has to play the role of an active listner and show due respect to their feelings, expressions and must develop mutual trust, even if it means moving slow and missing some aspects of their life that are important from the point of view of our topic of research. The life histories collected by me will be useful in understanding the perception of these women and the family strategies and the contribution these women have made to their family survival.

In addition, in the field work, attempts are made to obtain available documentary materials like official archival data, government gazetteers. Specially at Hospet, it was essential to establish the historical background as the Basavi practice is said to have flourished during the times of Vijayanagar empire. In Hampi, in the ruins of the capital, there is a separate street of the prostitutes and it is said when the Beda warrior community men left for war, the women were required to folllow this practice for perpetuating the family line. An extensive investigation into the land office records, is also felt necessary to understand the land acquisition and its impact on changing status of women in the community.

Tape-recorders and photographic equipment are some important supplemental items used in the field. In order to ensure accuracy and completeness I did tape record life history narratives but found transcribing materials from tapes to notes often tedious and time consuming task. Tape recorders are particularly useful in recording folk songs and folk tales while photography is useful in documenting complex events like rituals, celebrations etc.

In the light of the multiple modes of data collection in the field, I firmly believe that if we accept that getting the facts or developing a body of descriptive data on women's differential roles is an essential part of Women's Studies and if we want to dymistify women's invisibility and establish the factual reality of women's contribution to the working of the social system as a whole, we need studies with a more searching quest for realistic and valid information. Further, this information can come from women themselves by conducting first hand field-work in their natural life events and contexual situations. Thus, to me any research programme that strives to focus on empirical reality of women's issues and their concerns must necessarily involve the use of fieldwork. Hence, I consider training in first hand field-work method or participatory research a prerequisite for strengthening research capabilities of students in women's studies.

Finally, a few observations about the linkage between research and action, merit mention here as some scholars feel that in women's studies all academic research is to be necessarily linked to action oriented programme and a concern about its absence is often expressed. Firstly, while seeking linkage between research and action, let one not lose sight of the fact that in women's studies the researchers themselves are activists. The creation of new knowledge about the realities of women's life that we endeavour to produce through our empirical research is itself aimed at bringing a transformation in the values and attitudes of the society towards women. Creation of authentic knowledge and its dissemination through published work will go a long way in demystifying the myths about women. The very act of collecting life histories focussing on women and asking them to speak for themselves is a challenge to the traditional male-centred history.

In changing the course of our discipline, we are indeed performing the role of an activist. Being trained as academicians we are rejecting the very premises of the existing knowledge. Hence I do not mean to say that those of us who are engaged in academic pursuits should not take part in actual development work for the rural, tribal or down-trodden class if we feel we are capable of it. But let us not underestimate the contribution of academic research.

Secondly, when we think about action programmes for women's development, we will have to be very cautious. Because when we talk of development, the important questions we must consider is development from whose point of view? From the researcher's and planner's point of view or from the women's point of view. To give you an example a voluntary organization working for rural development thought that it wanted to start a school in the village, the lofty ideal was of course to educate the rural children. When this was proposed to the members of the Mahila Mandal, the women said if you really want to help us, instead of a sohool you get us a well in the village. Do you know why they asked for a well. The majority of the villagers belonged to labour class families and they knew that the children could not be dispensed and sent to school as earning a livelihood was necessary for everyone in the family including childern. So, the women preferred having a well in the village that would save them the drudgery of walking a distance of two miles every day to fetch water. Mind you, that is why there is the talk of participatory development. Sometimes it is more important to understand why a particular system works the way it does and what are the factors responsible for it and whether it is possible to bring a overall change. In the *devadasi* practice I know that the women are sexually exploited by the family and the community and there are a number of forces operating. Now even if I want the women to give up the practice I will have to think whether they really can give it up and if they give it up what other alternatives will they have and whether these alternatives will be a better choice. This I am saying because there is no single reason responsible for the *devadasi* custom and unless we bring to total structural change in the society, it probably may not be possible to eradicate it. But since in our efforts to ban it, laws are passed, many of the women have been forced to take to commercial prostitution and experience much lower status in the society as they are socially ostricised. Earlier, they were accepted by the community and suffered from no discrimination. What disaster can happen if we do not plan change or development properly is evident in-A case of Chandragutti. The social workers and police who tried to stop the nude worship were stripped of their clothes as a result of mob. So, to me it seems that our concern in women's studies should be to see that women are empowered to decide for themselves and make their own choices. And if we impose our views on other women, we too will be guilty of perpetuating the system.

While working for women's development, the academicians with the skills they have acquired can be helpful in different ways to the voluntary organizations and government agencies. 1. They can work as resource persons while programmes of development are chalked out by making it sure that women form a part of the programmes. 2. They can undertake basic research to make the complex reality evident. 3. They can undertake action-oriented research. 4. They can undertake evaluatory research studies for the voluntary organizations and the government agencies to assess the impact of development programmes on the target groups.

CHAPTER FIVE

Reconstructing Women's History: Problems and Paradigms

DR. P. SUDHIR

'After all, is there a problem ? And if so, What is it'

—Simone de Beauvoir,

The Second Sex

The first problem we encounter when we consider the reconstruction of Women's history is the question of necessity. Do we *need* women's history ? The necessity of women's history may be taken to be axiomatic.[1] Nevertheless, the question needs to be raised, not as a rhetorical device to fling a polemical answer in the face of critics from both sides of the gender gap, but as an explanatory tool which will enable us to illuminate and clarify other issues connected with the reconstruction of women's history. For, in attempting to understand why we need women's history, we can also understand how it should be reconstructed.

Why do we need women's history ? A simple but accurate answer would be that women, who hold up half the sky (as the Chinese proverb has it) have hitherto been left out of history, or when included, relegated to the periphery. There is, therefore, a need, it seems, to produce a history of women or a women's history. That the two are not the same is not a conundrum for Alice to unravel. The distinction will become clear perhaps when we seek to understand why women have hitherto been left out of history, One reason is that traditional historiography has tended to focus upon areas of human activity in which males were dominant. Politics, wars, the rise and fall of dynasties, such was the stuff of which traditional history was made, and in these, by definition, women had no role to play. Indeed, when on occasion women were allowed into the pages of history—Jhansi Laxmibai, John of Arc, Elizabeth I—it was because they were exceptional women, performing male roles.

Another reason, connected with the nrst, but more insiduous, and perhaps more significant, is that women have had no history because the expropriation of history is an important mechanism for reproducing, in the ideological sphere, social inequality. One need not go so far as to suggest that traditional concepts of history were engendered in the gender inequality. But there need not be any doubt that just as in the economic realm, relations of dominance and subordination are reinforced by the expropriation of the economic surplus, so too we can say, the expropriation of history from the women is a means of reinforcing male dominance.

In fact, the expropriation of hi tory from women facilitates the creation of a historical discourse which further reinforces gender inequality, even, sometimes while bring ng women into history. The creation of cultural stereotypes and the perpetuation of such stereotypes about women through an apparently scientific reconstruction of history is an example.[2]

If a struggle is to be waged against all structures of oppression and inequality to construct a more human and humane society, it is necessary not only to return women to history, but even more importantly, to return history to women.

How is this to be done ? Merely constructing a 'compensatory' history, to redress the balance, to counter centuries of neglect is, while necessary, not sufficient. In fact, this essential task has, in its execution, some inherent dangers. One is that the pursuit of the past as an end unto itself can become a substitute for changing the present.[3] Besides, there is the danger that there can be 'overcompensation', leading to a women's history which excludes men, whereas what we need is an inclusive history which is truly total in scope.[4] As Shiela Rowbotham puts it, 'simply studying women in the present does not necessarily question the whole scope of history. It could mean we study only exceptional women, or that we study only the political aspects of women's movements'.[5] There is the additional danger that in simply reconstructing Women's history, concepts, keywords and paradigms may be borrowed from a male oriented historical tradition, thus contributing to a distorted vision of women's lives in the past. This danger stems from the fact that women have been conditioned through several mediatory processes to view the world through categories of perception constructed by men,[6] It stems also from the very nature of historical knowledge that has hitherto been produced. Our knowledge of the past is critically determined by the significance we attach to historical facts and the way in which we decode historical texts, processes which are themselves historically conditioned.

We need, therefore a women's history which not merely adds to the fund of knowledge we have about women in past societies, but one which seeks to reformulate traditional concepts and categories. We need a women's history which is not satisfied with mere narrative, but one which will transform our view of history itself.

A striking example is the concept of 'work'. Early research (and some present research too) tended to focus on 'work' in the public sphere. It is only lately that it has been recognized that domestic work also is work and that it too bas a history. Again, traditional historiography has tended to see the spread of educational opportunities for women as an important historical phenomenon, thus accepting the idea that education is per se an instrument of social change. This in itself is debatable, especially after Gramsci and Paulo Freire. When the *content* of women's education is subjected to careful historical scrutiny, what we discover is that apart from implicit sexual stereotyping, the course structures themselves contributed to the reinforcement of culturally determined notions of femininity.[7]

But problems do not arise merely because terms or concepts are borrowed from a dominant tradition. They can arise even from within a radical and subversive tradition.

One of the most important of these is the question of patriarchy.

Patriarchy, and the relations of power embedded in it have been with us for a long time.[8] One need not accept the contention of Simone de Beauvoir that throughout history women have always been subordinated to men.[9] Nor does one need to accept the ideas of Shulasmith Firestone, for whom the sexual division and the consequent conflict are the main factors in history.[10] Nevertheless, it needs to be recognised that subordination of women appears to be virtually trans-historical, persisting through successive transformations of society. Attempts to reconstruct women's history cannot therefore skirt around the problem. It is a crucial problem for two reasons. Firstly, the relation of dominance and subordination inherent in patriarchy crucially shaped the contours of women's lives and even their knowledge of their lives. Secondly, it is necessary to understand how patriarchal structures operate and reproduce themselves, if we wish to dismantle them.

But the term 'patriarchy' poses its own problems, as Shiela Rowbotham points out. According to her the term implies, 'a universal and historical form of oppression which returns us to biology – and thus it obscures the need to recognise not only biological differences, but also the multiplicity of ways in which societies have defined gender'.[11] Besides, she argues, relations between men and women are also characterised by reciprocities and that we should not assume that the antagonism is a permanent feature.[12] Rosalind Coward has attacked the theory from another angle altogether. She suggests that as a concept, 'Patriarchy' originated in male debates about the roots and nature of society and that it cannot therefore serve to explain women's subordination.[13]

Part of the reluctance to grapple with the concept of patriarchy comes from the apparent failure of Marxism to provide an elaborate theoretical explanation of women's subordination. The centrality assigned in classical Marxism to class and class struggle means that the forms of exploitation which work through gender inequalities are untheorisable (class has no gender).[14]

The formulations of Engels, which constitute the major theoretical insights into women's subordination have been rejected by some historians as inadequate.[15]

While it is true that patriarchal power structures cannot simply be derived from property relations, and indeed, Maurice Godelior has brought to our attention sexual subordination in egalitarian societies, the concept has its uses. 'It points to a strategy which will elimiaate not men but masculinity, and transform the whole web of psycho-social relations in which masculinity and feminity are fromed'.[16]

While the debate on patriarchy is relevant to any discussion of women's history, what is of greater importance perhaps is the question of how patriarchy propagates itself. How is gender ideology produced and reproduced ? What are the mediatory mechanisms that facilitate the internalisation of ideology ? How is the consciousness of women shaped by the dominant discourse ? To answer of these questions, we may need to borrow from psycho-analysis, structuralist linguistics and discourse theory. But those questions need to be asked, because it is probably in the ideological realm that many of the crucial struggles of women have to waged.[17] The fact that patriarchal ideology seems to reinforce itself at points of transition, suggests that it may not be enough to overthrow the basic structures of exploitation. The struggle has to be waged on the ideological plane as well.

This is not to assign a status of autonomy to ideology, but to suggest that in focussing upon the material conditions of women's existence, one should not ignore the other dimensions of women's lives. The lives of women, like the lives of other members of society are rich and complex tissues. It is perhaps necessary to adopt, as Sumit Sarkar has suggested in a different context, the view points of anthropology (regarding culture) to create an 'integral history').[18]

Any discussion of subordination of women needs also to contend with the concept of 'oppression' which appears to confer a false sense of solidarity. Are women really sisters under the skin, bound together by the common oppression by men ? It needs to be recognised that oppression meant different things to different groups of women at different times.[19] The problem can be differently posed. Do women constitute a separate class by virtue of the fact that they are becoming conscious of being exploited ? While there is no difficulty in rejecting the idea that women can constitute a homogeneous class, it is important to be aware of the complex ways in which men and women are related, and how if the category of women is made too abstract, we will secure no useful results from historical inquiry.

Take, for example, the notion that women were marginalised, and pushed into the domestic, private sphere. This is a notion that is related to class. Working class women were not always so confined. Similarly, notions of sexuality, marriage and family are also functions of class.[20]

What is needed, therefore, is a theoretical framework in

which both gender inequality and class inequality are incorporated and their articulation examined. Otherwise, even in radical scholarship, the assumption can too easily be made that women are marginal. As Gayatri Chakravorty Spivak pointed out, "a feminist historian of the Subaltern must raise the question of women as structural rather than marginal isssues.[21]

More problematic than any lack of theoretical precision may be the question of sources. The reconstruction of women's history is made difficult because of the nature of available historical data. But this does not mean it renders the task virtuality impossible. On the contrary, the search for new kinds of sources, and even new areas of investigation have enriched our understanding of the historical process. Oral History has proved to be an important method for women's history, just as the search for women's autobiographical writings has unearthed a large number of such texts, and the search is on for more texts. But there are problems inherent in such sources, direct as they may seem to be. These texts, whether oral or written, are produced by women who have been conditioned to think and express in certain ways. Their discourse then has to be carefully decoded if the historian is to make meaningful use of it.[22] Structuralism tells us that there is no innocent text, and we are required to consider the ideological contexts in which texts are produced. The historian then has to attempt to escape the categories of thought in which the historical texts were conceived and produced. That is, it is not enough to collect the documents and hope to produce a narrative account of how felt or thought at a particular time. We need to place the texts in their contexts.

This is equally true of other kinds of sources such as literary texts or archaelogical artifacts. New ways of reading the texts or interpreting data have to be developed if, we wish to integrate women into history and not merely construct a narrative of women in history.

De-emphasising the narrative element in history is not to ask for its total exclusion. What is being suggested is the need for searching for new ways of interpreting historical data, for new concepts. Research then needs to focus upon issues that relate to women and their interaction with the productive process, rather than upon questions that are only apparently women's issues. We need to know, no doubt how women acted in times of war or political crisis, and how the problems of women participating in a mass movements are different from those of men, but we need to go beyond these studies of 'roles' to considerations of the ways in which the world of women mental and the material is constructed, how women perceive transitions in society.

Women's History has already begun to transform the manner in which we perceive the past. Just as it is no longer possible to consider patriarch only in terms of property relations, it is perhaps difficult to consider modes of production divorced from the domestic sphere and the family. Women's history has also helped to focus attention of historians on areas hitherto ignored. If these are its only achievements, women's history will perhaps remain another sub-discipline. But in the end, its true purpose and aim is to explore structures of oppression and by exploring them, to end them.

REFERENCES

1. For a brief, but lucid discussion of this question, see Kameshwari J and Rekha Pande, 'The Need for Women's History,' *Proceedings of the AP History Congress*, 11th Session 1986.

2 Aloka Parasher, 'Nationalist Historians and the creation of Cultural Stereotypes in History' Mimeographed paper presented to Seminar on 'Women in a Changing Society', Hyderabad, 1986.

3. Shiela Rowbotham, *Hidden from History : Rediscovering Women in History from the 17th Century to the Present*, New York, 1976; p. xx.

4. For a discussion of the idea of 'total history', see Peter Burke, 'People's History or Total History' in Raphael Samuel (ed). *People's History and Socialist Theory*, London 1981, pp 4-9.

5. Shiela Rowbotham, *op. cit.*, p. xxi.

6. See Mary Beth Norton, 'Is Clio a Feminist ? The New History', *New York Times Book Review*, 13 April 1986.

7. Rousseau had this to say for example, in *Emile* : Thus women's entire education should be placed in relation to men. To please men, to be useful to them, to win their love and respect, to raise them as children, care for them as adults...Interestingly, 19th century social reformers, men *and* women, in India echoed similar ideas on women's education.

8. For an interesting discussion of this, see Maurice Godolier, 'The Origins of Male Domination', *New Left Review*, 127 (1981) pp 3-17.

9. Simone de Beauvoir, *The Second Sex*, p xviii.

10. Shulasmith Firestone, *The Dialectic of Sex*, London, 1972.

11. Shiela Rowbotham, 'The Trouble with Patriarchy' in Raphael Samuel (ed) *People's History and Socialist Theory*, pp 364-69.

12. *Ibid*.

13. Rosalind Coward, *Patriarchal Precedents : Sexuality and Social Relations*, London 1983.

14. Ted Benton, *The Rise and Fall of Structural Marxism : Althusser and his Influence*, London, 1984, pp . 134-40.

15. Ann J. Lane, 'Women in Society ; A Critique of Frederick Engels' in Berenice Carroll (ed.) *Liberating Women's History : Theoretical and Critical Essays*, Urbana, 1976, pp. 4-25.

16. Sally Alexander and Barbara Taylor 'In Defence of Patriarchy' in. Raphael Samuel (ed.) *People's History and Socialist Theory*,pp 370-73.

17. See Michele Barrett, *Women's Oppression Today : Problems in Marxist Feminist Analysis*, London, 1980, pp. 84-113.

18. Sumit Sarkar, 'Social History : Predicaments and Possibilities, 'Presidential Address, Modern India Section, Indian History Congress, 1984.

19. Ann D. Gordon, Mari Jo Buhle, and Nancy Schrom Dye, 'The Problem of Women's History' in Berenice Carroll (ed.) *Liberating Women's History*, pp. 75-92.

20. See for example, Lawrence Stone, *The Family Sex and Marriage in England, 1500-1800*, Harmondsworth, 1979.

21. Gayatri Chakravorty Spivak, 'Subaltern Studies: De constructing Historiography' in R. Guha (ed.) *Subaltern Studies IV*, pp. 330-363.

22. Susie Tharu 'Oral History, Narrative Strategy and the Figures of Autobiography', Mimeographed Paper presented to the Seminar on Narrative, University of Hyderabad.

CHAPTER SIX

The Challenge of Women's History

DR. KUMKUM ROY

> "In order to write a new history worthy of the name, we will have to recognise that no single methodological and conceptual framework can fit the complexities of the historical experience of all women." (Lerner 1979 : 158).

The study of women's history is a field which has been assuming increasing significance in recent times. What is noteworthy about this development is the interpenetration of purely academic approaches with activist concerns, so much so that at times the academic activist dichotomy seems irrelevant. Thus, to a great extent, the study of our past has been visualised as a means of understanding the sources of our oppression and hence of removing them. This perspective has proved extremely fruitful, both in terms of theoretical insights, as well as in terms of detailed empirical studies. Another perspective, which has also served to enrich the field, is typified by Mary R. Beard, who viewed women as "active agents in the world, shaping their own destinies within restricted possibilities, resisting and overthrowing these restrictions and sometimes even acting in complicity with the forces that keep them in a state of social inferiority" (DuBois *et al.* 1985 : 39). In practice, these perspectives are by no means mutually exclusive. Here, we will focus on some of the major theoretical approaches which have emerged as a result of the on-going debate amongst feminist scholars, as well as on some of the insights which have emerged from specific studies. The survey which follows is illustrative rather than comprehensive.

The starting point for women's history is the assumption that although men and women are biologically different, what is historically significant is that women constitute a social as opposed to a biological group. According to some scholars such as Smith (1976 : 369) this social group has a certain unity in that "it has experienced both overt and covert controls through legal, political and social restrictions" While this is to an extent true, "the situation of women is different from that of any other social group" (Mitchell 1984 : 18). Further the complexity of women's situations must constantly be borne in mind. For example, while the oppression of women has obviously taken different forms for different social groups within the same society, the position of women and men within the same social group has usually been markedly different. Thus, analogies with racism and colonialism, though useful in focussing on certain common features such as the internalisation of the perceptions of the oppressors by the victims remain analogies (Kelly-Gadol 1976). Women's oppression is by no means identical with other systems of oppression, though these may mutually reinforce one another. Further, while there are certain common elements in women's oppression, irrespective of time and place, the specificities of each situation need to be understood and analysed.[1]...As Brown (1981 : 254) observes :

> "The notion of "woman" has to be interpreted *within* the parameters and definitions meaningful to the society that does the (social) constructing.

> There is no essence of woman distinct from the definition of "Woman" within a society, and if a theory of patriarchy is to be developed which does not fly in the face of ethnographic fact, it will have to confront the variety and complexity of such definitions of "woman" with a great deal of subtlety and sensitivity" (italics original).

Such concerns have stimulated considerable theoretical discussion.[2] One of the possibilities which have been explored, refined and followed up with concrete research is that postulated by Engels in the *Origin of the family, Private Property and the State*, linking women's oppression with changes in the economic and political realm. This perspective is particularly fruitful from the historical point of view as it assumes that women's oppression is a historical feature rather than a universal and eternal phenomenon. It has also led to a considerable amount of research on social divisions in classless societies by scholars such as Leacock (1981), and while the evidence is by no means uniform as there are gender differences if not stratification in such societies, a wealth of new data is now available.

Attempts have also been made to refine the theory by incorporating features such as the growth of trade and warfare and changes in religious beliefs (Rapp, 1977). Further, the solution of women's oppression which Engles proposes. viz the increasing participation of women in productive activities, has been questioned. Thus, scholars such as Friedl (1975) have pointed out that, apart from women's role in production, what is probably crucial in determining access to power is "control over the distribution of goods outside the household", as there are societies where women are the major producers but do not exercise control over the fruits of their labour. As Brown (1981) observes : "Slaves after all. may perform the bulk of productive tasks in a society". This debate has been useful in focussing on the complexities of the sexual division of labour and on the need to widen the definitions of economically relevant activities.

A second approach starts with a view of universal female subordination related to women's capacity for biological reproduction and the connected risk of child bearing. While this is a debatable proposition, this approach has proved of crucial significance because of its

> "ability to bring issues like domesticity, child-bearing and motherhood to the centre of explanations for sexual hierarchy and to the fore-front of social analysis in general". (DuBois *et. al*, 1985 : 97).

This perspective is also useful in focussing on the demarcation between private and public spheres and in attempting to assess the significance of such divisions for women. Attempts have also been made to understand when this demarcation began. Draper (1975) for instance associates it with the beginning of Permanent Settlements associated with agriculture, an argument in many ways implicit in Boserup's studies of the shift from horticulture to agriculture. However, others such as Reiter (1975) link it to the beginnings of industrial capitalism. This has been further refined by Barrett (1980 : 165) who argues that while the separation becomes important with the emergence of capitalism, it owes it specific characteristics to a precapitalistic ideology of gender. More specific studies, such as Hall's (1982) examine how and why this demarcation evolves in 19th century England and its impact on middle-class women. Further, while some scholars such as Goody have argued that the demarcation is beneficial to women as it allows them a sphere of influence and control, others argue that such differentiation is a distinct source of oppression when the women's sphere is devalued in the total social order.[3]

It has also been suggested (eg; Stanley 1981) that women's role as child-bearers and rearers limits their ability to participate actively in production and hence is responsible for their oppression. However, other scholars such as Friedl (1975) argue that the time spent by women in child care is determined by their role is subsistence rather than the former determining the latter. This is useful in drawing attention to the fact that there may not be a one-way relationship between roles reproduction and production. Once again, the potential for future research is obvious. The complex links between the domestic and public domain and attempts to enforce and challenge such demarcations remain to be explored in the context of Indian history.

Related in a sense to this approach, but having the advantage of being less biologically deterministic, is the concept of gender. Perhaps one of the most succinct definitions of gender has been offered by Rubin (1975 : 159) who regards it as :

> "a set of arrangements by which a society transforms biological sexuality into products of human activity and in which these transformed sexual needs are satisfied".

It also implies "obligatory heterosexuality and the constraint of female sexuality" (*Ibid* : 179) in most historical situations. Rubin also suggests that :

> "the division of labour by sex can be seen as a taboo, against the sameness of men and women, a taboo dividing the sexes into two mutually exclusive categories, a taboo which exacerbates the biological differences between the sexes and there by *creates* gender" (emphasis original).

Rubin further argues that sexual systems may have a certain autonomy and may not be directly correlated to economic changes.

The concept of gender implies that masculine and feminine characteristics are socially imposed and not biologically inevitable. This is evident from the fact that the specific elements regarded as crucial to definitions of masculinity and feminity vary considerably over space and time.

Some attempts to synthesise these diverse perspectives are also evident, as for instance in socialist-feminist analyses of housework, the domestic labour required to reproduce, biologically and socially the labour force in capitalist society. Such analyses, while focussing on the centrality of the economy in influencing developments in other spheres, also draw attention to the links between the situation within the household and that without, and include attempts to evaluate the economic sifinificance of housework., which are clearly influenced by radical feminist concerns regarding the domestic and public spheres.

While some of the scholarship which has emerged from a realisation of the importance of treating women as a distinct category attempts to utilise had refine these new conceptual frameworks, the tendency of fitting women into pre-existing frameworks persists. But simplistically this consists in showing that women also did the things men did. This, while useful in unearthing information, often has overlooked, has certain limitations as well and has come in for criticism, especially from Lerner (1979) who points out the limitations of criteria which determine success and failure by masculine yardsticks, and thus overlooks the possibility of a different yardstick being valuable from the feminine point of view. The assessment of success or victimisation which emerges from this stand point may provide only a partial assessment of the situation. An example of the former tendency according to Lerner (*Ibid*: 147) is the view of Margaret Sanger as the founder of the birth control movement. However, she could also be viewed :

> "as a woman raising a revolutionary challenge to the centuries old practice by which the bodies and lives of women are dominated and ruled by man made laws." (*Ibid*)

Apart from individual women's lives being distorted, very often the lives of entire groups of women are subjected to such male oriented analyses. Thus, the idealisation of the "cult of true womanhood" in mid-nineteenth century America, as depicted in the media, has been taken to reflect the actual restrictions on women. However, Lerner (*Ibid* : 149) argues that "idealism is very frequently a defensive ideology and an expression of tension within society", and that in fact both lower class and middle class women were challenging the situation in which they were challenging the situation in which they were placed.

In a sense, the limitations of "contributory history" are related to the problem of sources. As Smith (1976:372) observes:

> "If women had a separate existence then the search for their materials must work from an awareness of that separation. Historical materials are preserved when it is in someone's interest to preserve them."

Much of the literature that has been handed down to us is the work of men. and obviously reflects their perspective on women. Further, we must recognise the possibility that some of the works of women which survive, may do so because these are women who have accepted the masculine canons of the day and become as it were, "one of the boys".[4] There is also the problem of whether the women who leave behind written records are typical or not. As Dyhouse (1981 : 31) observes:

> "It is often easier for the historian to find out about the attitudes and experiences of those women who rejected conventional expectations and shaped their lives accordingly. The latter group was less likely to leave autobiographies or other written records or to inspire biographies".

although she cautions that :

> "we must certainly be careful not to fall into the trap of assuming that because women were silent about their lives they accepted the conventions, let alone rested happy or content with the existing order of things (*Ibid*, italics original).

A further problem related to textual sources is the reluctance of male scholars (who are both numerically preponderant and almost universally regarded as authorities), to recognise works conventionally ascribed to women as being the actual works of women. Thus, in the early Indian context, Neumann, who edited the Therigatha or the songs of the Buddhist nuns concluded that these must "have been shaped by a man." Fortunately, Rhys Davids, who translated the text, refuted this hypothesis effectively.[5]

Sometimes, the ascription of the works of women to men is done on the flimsiest of grounds. For instance, there is a commentary in the *Yajnavalkys Smrti* which is ascribed to Balambhatta. According to Vidyarnava (1918 : iii) the translator of the text,

> "the book professes to have been composed by a learned lady but Babu Govinda Dasa of Benares, the learned editor of the *Editio Princeps* of Balambhatti States that the real author of it was the husband of this lady. The author Vaidyanatha Paiyagunda lived in the 18th century, and as he lived in Benares, there is every reason to believe in the truth of this Benares tradition".

Vidyarnava does not even pause to consider why this scholar should have adopted the rather unusual expedient of using his wife's name. One cannot help but wonder that if the case had been otherwise, i.e. a man had been named as the author, whether his work would have been as easily ascribed to his wife or not. What is amply evident is that in our search for women's voices from the past, we must be constantly alert to the possibility of the appropriation of women's work, especially by male scholars of the 19th and 20th centuries, for many of whom traditional patriarchal values were reinforced by the ideals of western patriarchy.

Despite these limitations, recent feminist scholarship illustrates the possibilities which arise from looking at old sources afresh, from a different perspective and with new questions in mind. Here, I will deliberately focus on two rather early periods of history, as the problem of sources for history in general and for Women's history in particular, grow particularly acute the further we go back in time. The first example is Barstow's analysis of the archaeological evidence from Catal Huyuk, a neolithic settlement of the Anatolian Plateau. She demonstrates (1978) how a culture which was extremely complex, materially rich (in terms of textiles, wooden and clay vessels, stone tools, agriculture, pastoralism and trade) evolved and existed for over a thousand years without a clearly evolved social and political hierarchy. She links this to the fact that the social organisation appears to have been women centred, with the cult of the goddess providing a certain unifying ideology. What is also interesting is that the excavator, Mellaart, on whose work Barstow relies, himself had an ambiguous, if not, positively hostile attitude towards the evidence he encountered. For instance, he refers to the males at Catal Huyuk as "not as yet being subject to the wiles of women" (cited in Barstow). Nonetheless, he appears to have faithfully recorded his finds, thus making possible a reinterpretation of the evidence.[6]

Other scholars such as Rohrlich (1980) have re-examined Sumerian myths and legal codes, including the code of Hammurabi, to focus on the connections between the growing subordination of women, the destruction of clan egalitarianism and the emergence of the state in Sumer. The changing status of women she argues, is often reflected in the changing status of goddesses. One striking example is that of Nisaba, the goddess of reeds, who during the earliest period, was referred to as the patron goddess of scribes, and was associated with accounting, science, education and the invention of the script. However, by the time of Hammurabi, she was replaced by Nabu, the son of the supreme war-god, Marduk. The latter, incidentally acquires his position through killing the goddess Tiamat, earlier regarded as the mother of creation, but later conceived of as the embodiment of chaos. The ritual enactment of the killing of Tiamat, moreover, was part of the annual new year day celebrations by the 18th century B.C. Rohrlich also argues that Hammurabi's law code, which has often been thought of as a means of guaranteeing the rights of women, in reality probably curtailed their opportunities by strictly delimiting the spheres within which they could legitimately function. Such analyses demonstrate that despite the problem of sources, the limitations of "contributory history can be overcome."

This is mainly owing to the fact that the perspectives discussed earlier have opened up a number of new areas for investigation. It is now generally recognised for instance, that analyses of women's oppression which trace its origin and perpetuation to the superior physical force of men are simplistic.[7] Hence, considerable attention has been given to the process of socialisation (eg Dyhouse 1981) which examines how the characteristics of masculinity and feminity are transmitted from one generation to another.[8]

Linked to the process of socialisation are studies of the groups of sexual ideologies which are thus transmitted. While the specific content of a sexual ideology are obviously important. Dwyer (1978) suggests that there are four theoretically possible kinds of acceptance which such an ideology may enjoy; one in which men and women hold the same ideas about maleness and femaleness, the second in which they agree about maleness, but disagree about femaleness, the third in which they agree about femaleness but disagree about maleness and the fourth where they disagree about both. According to her, an understanding of sexual ideology is useful in any analysis of women's consciousness, and in studying the forms of action open to them in any particular situation. As historians, I would suggest we should also examine the possibilities of change from one kind of acceptance to another and study how and why this comes about as well as the consequences of such changes.

Attempts have also been made to analyse the variety of forms in which women's resistance to and anger against the situation in which they were placed may have manifested itself. Thus, it is widely recognised that such "female diseases" like hysteria are a form of expressing resentment often used, perhaps subconsciously, by women, to disrupt a situation which is perceived of as being oppressive.

At a different level, women's "innately quarrelsome" nature often disguises a strategy for acquiring power. According to Collier (1974) in societies organised along patrilineal lines, the interest of men and women in the kinship structure are different. Men exercise greater control in situations where the lineage is consolidated, whereas women exercise covert power at least where the lineage breaks up. Thus, women who attempt to disrupt the male lineage by quarrelling are not simply being petty. but are actually trying to obtain control over at least some aspects of their lives in a situation weighed heavily against them. Such analyses are useful in sensitising us to the need to search for newer meanings to much of women's individual and collective behaviour which has been taken for granted.

As noted earlier, some historians have also attempted to study women as agents of history within what are overtly oppressive systems. One of the most striking examples of the potential of such scholarship is provided by Angela Davis' account of black women in slavery. As DuBois *et. al* point out (1985 : 50-51):

> "By treating black women as active agents rather than passive victims in this most oppressive of American institutions, Davis helped to forge a new approach to the history of both slavery and women. Instead of focussing on the big house and slave field, where the whites were in control, she gave her attention to the slave quarters, where women helped to develop an maintain and independent Afro-American Culture."

Feminist scholarship has also focussed attention on the need to re-examine the nature of the family. Many earlier sociological and anthropological studies tended to treat the family as a homogeneous unit, often identified ideally with its male head. However, recent studies have revealed that "there is nothing inevitable about the form or role of the family any more than there is about the character or role of women" (Mitchell 1985 : 18-19). Thus we need to study the life-cycles of both men and women within the family, recognising that these are culturally conditioned.

It is also evident that biological and social units do not

necessarily coincide. Thus, in many societies, the biological and social parents are different. Amongst the Nuer in Africa, for instance, the biological father is not recognised (Edholm, 1982 : 173) and the social father may be a biological female. Incest taboos, likewise, though almost universal, vary remarkably in the actual specifications of the kin. Hence, we need to be sensitive to structures other than the male headed nuclear family which has often unquestioningly been accepted as the norm.

Further, the possibility of conflict within the family is receiving greater attention as an issue of academic concern. Hartmann (1981 : 368) for instance, points out that while the family may be a unit in which both production and redistribution take place, the interests of members of this unit are by no means identical. This realisation can lead to a fuller history of the family which takes into consideration the structural elements of intra-familial tension instead of dismissing these as personal problems.

Related to the family structure is the institution of marriage and the consequent regulation of female sexuality and reproductive abilities. Here we need to examine the specific features and functions associated with marriage in particular social contexts. According to Comer (1982 : 180) for example, in western capitalist societies, marriage is important as a form of social control. She says :

> "without marriage as the private safety valve for public conflict, women would not tolerate the injustices of unequal pay, power and education and the degradation of sexual objectification—all the things, in fact, which make up the sum total of their usefulness...Marriage is presented as society's panacea for these ills. Marriage does not solve these conflicts, but the fact that it contains them, is what makes it such an effective and useful form of social control."

We also need to understand how and why women's sexuality is controlled and restricted both within and outside the frame-work of marriage and the varying nature of the restrictions on male and female sexuality. Barrett (1980 : 72) for example argues that from a patriarchal perspective, the need to control and harness female sexuality for physical reproduction is possibly greater as "the connection for *men* between sexuality and procreation is much closer than it is for women." (italics original). Here again we need to explore the social construction which emerge on the basis of this physiological difference.

Studies on the significance attached to biological reproduction in any particular society and the degree of control women exercise over it are also illuminating. An example of the possibilities in this sphere is provided by Weiner's (1976) study of the Trobriand islanders. According to her, men and women share political and economic power in Trobriand society, whereas women have full control over reproduction and this provides them with a very real source of power. She also illustrates how earlier scholars like Malinowski conditioned by western sexist values, failed to perceive the power exercised by women. In this instance, women's power in a particular sphere, reinforces their control in other spheres as well. However, the relation between production and reproduction may not be so simple in every case. Nevertheless, focussing on such connections will enable us to arrive at a historical analysis which will possess greater depth and validity than the current practice of confining analyses to the public sphere of production alone.

In some other cases, the control women exercise over the very process of child birth may be at stake. This is especially true of contemporary western capitalist societies (Graham and Oakley, 1982) where the perceptions of pregnant women and those of medical experts differ markedly, with the latter having far greater control over the process than the former. Studies of the reproductive process in such situations are especially useful in challenging accepted definitions of what is "natural" and "scientific" and illustrate the extent to which such concepts are socially conditioned.

At another level, rising or falling birth rates become matters of concern for those in authority and women may be coerced or persuaded to produce more or less children. Thus, "there is a considerable recent history of interventionist concern with reproduction on the part of socialist, capitalist and fascist states (Riley 1981 : 189). We need to understand who attempts to control such processes and how and why this occurs. As Greenwood and king (1982 : 168-69) point out :

> "Generally speaking, the extent and openness with which birth control is practised is as much dependent on a society's attitude to sex and the status of women, as it is on technology. For the use of birth control requires a morality that permits the separation of sexual intercourse from procreation, and is related to the extent to which women are valued for roles other than just those of wife and mother."

The forms which the regulation of reproduction takes are also worthy of study. These may range from persuasion and social pressure to legislation and physical coercion. How women respond to such attempts must also be analysed. We must also remember that women's control over reproduction should not be measured simply in terms of access to birth control but in terms of a genuine freedom of choice to decide whether or not to have a child.

We also need to examine the specific history of motherhood, the process of rearing and socialising children, which far from being a natural fuuction of women, shows remarkable variation over space and time. As Antonis (1981) observes:

> "It is important to ask where the use of the phrase "maternal instinct" originated and how it was used, where the term has currency and whether it is useful."

We need to remember, for example as she points out, that "MATERNAL INSTINCT (as a good thing) is ASCRIBED TO MARRIED WOMEN ONLY!" (Capitals original).

Apart from such new areas of investigation one of the interesting insights which have emerged from recent studies is that the "golden ages" of history do not necessarily coincide for men and women. In fact the golden age of the one may be an age of decline for the other. Kelly Gadol (1976) was amongst the earliest to question the assumption that women's and men's statuses change in the same direction. Her own work indicates that there was a decline in the status of women during the renaiassance in Europe and during the American Revolution, both periods during which there was considerable progress from the point of view of mankind. Conversely, according to Smith (1976 : 384)

> "women gain most from periods of social dysfunction such as war or rebellion in which the normal connections of power are severed".

In the Indian context, the parallel which immediately springs to mind is the studies of the developmental process during the post-independence phase, which indicate the development may have accentuated the difference in status between the sexes. Such analyses suggest fresh questions for earlier phases of Indian History as well and pose a challenge for the accepted periodisation of history.

Most of the studies referred to above focus on the nature of the relationship between men and women. Some other studies however, focus exclusively on the relationships between women. Such relationships may take the form of support networks to handle "personal" crises or organisations for social welfare activities. Very often, the values which underlie such relationships are different from those which permeate male-female or male-male interaction. Historians and students of literature have evolved the category of women's culture or sub-culture to encompass such relationships. Originally used in the context of the relationship amongst white, literate women of 19th and 20th century Europe and America, the concept of women's cultury can possible be extended to other areas as well. For example in the Indian context, many craft traditions have been handed down from mother to daughter. It would be interesting to see the extent to which such traditions reflect a pattern which is different from the dominant tradition.

Despite this potential, it must be noted that the concept of a women's culture is not problem-free. As DuBois *et. al* asks (1985 : 66) :

> "What Value do we place on the cultures and traditions that women have created ? Do we discover so much strength and richness that our previous perceptions of subordination and inequality are all but eclipsed ? Or do we see women's separate work as making a poor virtue of necessity ? These are the poles of the debate; possible resolutions fall along a wide spectrum between them."

What is important is to be aware of the possibility of the existence of women's cultures and to assess the significance of each specific culture in terms of the context to which it is related.

It is evident therefore that the potentials inherent in reconstruction women's history are immense. Once we accept the challenge of recovering our past in all its camplexity, it is also likely that more questions well emerge, more theoretical refinements will be possible, and history in general will be enriched. To make this endeavour a success, we must be prepared to question many, if not, all of the accepted assumptions of our discipline, the definition of what is regarded as historically significant, for instance, and at the same test our new formulations against as wide a base of evidence as possible, recognising, in particular, the validity of the lived experiences of women, no matter how diverse these may be.

I would like to end by remembering Punna or Punnika, one of our less well-known foremothers, who exemplifies the qualities which would be required of the new historian. Punna, according to her biography in the *Therigatha*, was a serving girl, who later rose to be a Buddhist nun. The story runs, that one day, when she was still a poor serving girl, she went to the icy cool river on a winter morning to fetch water for the house hold where she was employed. She had obviously no means of escaping from this unpleasant task, but was quite surprised to see a Brahmana taking a purificatory bath in the river. Despite the obvious social distance between them, she does not hesitate to question him with a logic grounded in practical experience, and in a language whose clarity survives even in translation. Her song, as recorded in the *Therigatha* runs as follows ;

"Nay now, who, ignorant to the ignorant
Hath told thee this : that water-baptism
From evil *Karma* can avail to free ?
Why then the fishes and the tortoises,
The frogs, the water snakes, crocodiles
And all that haunt water straight to heaven
Will go......
And if these streams could bear away erst
Of evil thou hast wrought, they's bear away
They merit too, leaving thee stripped and bare.
That dreading which, thou, brahmana comest e'er
To bathe and shiver here, that, even that
Leave thou undone and save they skin from frost."

With women like Punna as our predecessors, we should be able to face the challenges before us.

NOTES

1. As DuBois *et. al* observe (1985 : 124-25) :

"the challenge in developing a theory of women's

oppression is to explain the extraordinary differences in Women's position and yet account for the astonishing persistence and continuity of some kind of subordination."

2. Much of the subsequent discussion is based on DuBois *et. al* (1985).

3. Lerner also cities the case of Jane Addams to illustrate clearly the divergence between her achievements from a masculine point of view which would be assessed in terms of social work, and her achievements from the female point of view, where her contribution to evolving a system of "living and working for a new generation of independent, educated women of the late 19th century who chose not to marry" was probably of greater significance.

4. This possibility was suggested to me by Professor Devahuti, Delhi University, in the context of later Vedic literature.

5. Her response runs as follows (Rhys Davids, 1948 : xxiii) :

> "Not often since the patriarchal age set in, has woman succeeded in so breaking through her barriers as to set on lasting record the expression of herself and of things as thèy appeared to her. But to assume that because this happened seldom, therefore, this collection of documents, though ascribed to her are necessarily not by her, is to carry over-far the truth : 'He that hath, to him shall be given and she that hath not, from her shall be taken even that which she hath'. I make no counter assumption that the gifted Theris had a hand in the compilation of the Brothers 'Psalms. I would only ask English readers to await the appearance of those, and note the interesting differences in idiom, sentiment and tone between them and the sisters 'Psalms. Even the 'common stock' of refrains is different."

6. As Mitchell (1984 : 30) observes,

"Physical deficiency is not new, any more than in the past, a sufficient explanation of women's relegation to inferior status.
Coercion has been ameliorated to an ideology shared by both sexes."

7. For a discussion of theories which attempt to explain how knowledge of gender is transmitted, see Kessler and Mc Kenna (1982).

8. I have retained Rhys Davids' (1948 : 117-118) translation on account of its authenticity, despite the somewhat archaic English.

REFERENCES

Antonis, B. 1981. Motherhood and Mothering in *Women in Society*, the Cambridge Women's Studies Group, London : Virago Press, pp. 55-74.

Barrett, M, 1980. *Women's oppression Today*. London : Verso
Barstow, A. 1978. The Uses of Archaeology for women's History : Jame's Mellaart's work on the Neolithic Mother Goddess at Catal Huyuk in Feminist Studies Vol 4, pp. 7-18.

Brown, P. 1981. Universals and Particulars in the position of women in *Women in Society*, pp. 242-56.

Collier, J. 1974. Women in Politics in *Women, Culture and Society* ed, Michelle Z Rosaldo and Louise Lamphere (Stanford : Stanford University Press).

Comer, L. 1982. Monogamy, marriage and economic dependence in *The Changing Experience of Women* (ed) E, Whitelegg et al, Oxford ; the Open University, pp. 178-189.

Davis, Angela, 1972. Reflections on the Black Women's Role in the Community of slaves. *Massachusetts Review* pp. 81-100.

Draper, P. 1975. Kung Women : Contrasts in Sexual Egalitarianism n Foraging and Sedentary Contexts in Reiter (ed) *Towards an Anthroipology of Women*. New York : Monthly Review Press, pp. 77-109.

Du Bois, Gail Paradise Kelly, Elizabeth Lapovsky Kennedy Carolyn Korsmeyer and Lillian S. Robinson. 1985 *Feminist Scholarship*. Urbana and Chicago : University of Illinois Press. Dwyer, D. 1978. Ideologies of Sexual Inequality and Strategies for Change in Male-Female Relations. American Ethnologist Vol 5, pp. 227-40.

Dykhuse, C. 1981. *Girls Growing Up in Late Victorian and Edwardian England.* London : Routledge and Kegan Paul. Edholm, F. 1982. The unnatural family in *The Changing Experience of Women* pp. 166-677.

Engels, F. 1972. *The Origin of the Family, private property and the State.* New York ; International Publishers.

Friedl, E. 1975. *Women and Men : An Anthropologist's view.* New York: Holt, Rinehart and Winston.

Greenwood, K. and L. King. 1981. Contraception and Abortion. in *Women in Society*. pp 168-184.

Graham, H. and A Oakley, 1982. Competing ideologies of reproduction ; medical and maternal perspectives on pregnancy in *The Changing Experience of Women* pp. 309-326.

Hall C. 1982. The butcher, the baker, the candlestickmaker : the shop and the family in the Industrial Revolution in *The Changing Experience of Women*. pp 2-16.

Hartmann, H, 1981. The family as the locus of gender, class and political struggles : the example of housework. Sings Vol 6, pp. 366-94. Kelly* Gadol, J. 1976. The Social Relation of the Sexes : Methodological Implications of Women's history *Signs* Vol I pp. 809-24.

Kessler, S. and W Mc Kenna. 1982. Developmental Aspects of Gender in *The Changing Experience of Women* pp. 297-285.

Leacock, E. 1981. *The Myth of Male Domination.*

Lerner, G. 1979, *The Majority Finds its Past.* New York : OUP

Mitchell, J. 1984. *Women : the Longest Revolution.* London : Virago Press.

Rap, R. 1977. Gender and Class : An Archaeology of knowledge concerning the origin of the state. *Dialectical Anthropology* Vol 2 pp. 109-30.

Reiter, R.R. 1975. *Introduction to Towards an Anthropology of Women* pp. 11-19.

Rhys Davids, C.A.F. (tr) (1948). *The Psalms of the Sisters.* London : the Pali Text Society.

Riley, D. 1981. Feminist Thought and Reproductive Control : the State and the right to choosed, in *Women in Society*, pp. 185-199.

Rubin, G. 1975. The Traffic in Women : Notes on the "Political Economy" of Sex in *Towards an Anthropology of Women* pp 157-210.

Smith, H. 1976. Feminism and the Methodology of Women's History in B. Carroll (ed) *Liberating Women's History*. Urbana : University of Illinois Press pp 368-384.

(Vidyarnava, S. (tr) 1918) *Yajnavalkya Smrti* Allahabad. Panini Office.

Weiner, A. 1976. *Women of Value, Men of Renown*. New perspectives on Trobriand Exchange, Austin : University of Texas Press.

CHAPTER SEVEN

Towards a Historiography of Women in People's Struggles:

SOME QUESTIONS ARISING FROM A STUDY OF WOMEN IN THE TELANGANA PEOPLE'S MOVEMENT OF THE 1940's

DR. SUSIE THARU

It is a chastening experience, as one begins to reflect on the question of women's history, to think back to one's school-text books. Etched into our memories are the beautiful Mumtaz Mahal which moved Shah Jahan to build the Mahal, and the brave Rani Laxmibhai of Jhansi who fought to retain her husband's kingdom. The only women who crossed those pages were the women great men loved, or those who through some accident of circumstance could enter fields customarily reserved for upper-class men.

Women's history as it has taken shape today grows out of the sudden recognition, precipitated by the women's movement, that such history not only marginalises women but mythologies them into a male centred world. Indeed, the life and work of the majority of women were systematically obscured by histories that purported to be factual or neutral. By and large this was as true of social history as it was of orthodox political history. Women's history then, is an intervention. It's intent political, not archival. It is an assertion that women have a history although that history has been distorted, even erased by the biases that pervade our culture and our scholarship. It is striking that much of this work is nurtured either outside the University, or on its fringes. As we search out and record these histories, we set out to reclaim a past and celebrate a lineage of resistance and growth, for to be deprived of a past is to inherit an impoverished present and future sealed off from change.

In Europe and America the very earliest work in the field was simply compensatory. The task was perceived as having to locate, and place alongside the great men of history, the great women who had been left out. Historians men with such success—women whose lives and whose work has been forgotten (or supressed) were "found" in surprising numbers in every walk of life—that attention was initially deflected from the fact that the resulting history remained a history of exceptional women. If we were to attempt a compensatory history of the Telangana Struggle, for instance, we would have located women who had acquired distinction within the movement. We would have recorded their achievement, stressing their heroism, their courage, their quality as fighters and organisers; in other words, their claim to a place withthe men.

While such efforts undoubtedly have value, the critique provided by compensatory history, is obviously not radical enough. Traditional history was forced to extend itself and accommodate more women. But the cultural biases, the political commitments and the disciplinary strategies that excluded women in the first place remained invisible, unquestioned, consequently intact. Women's absence from history, compensatory practices indicate, is an omission which can be set right with a little good will and application. Consequently, not only are women as a whole still hidden in these histories but the politics of oppression is completely obscured. Obviously women's history is no more an "addition" to mainstream history than labour or social history is an addition to the old political histories.

In India, women's history has developed in a some-what different mode. Initial efforts at what may seriously be regarded women's history were contributory histories. The emphasis in such studies shifts from documenting the achievements of notable women to describing and assessing the quality and extent of women's participation in, say, the social reform movement or the Satyagraha struggles. The questions that are asked now are, what did women, singly and as a whole, contribute to the movement; what was their status in it; and sometimes, even, how did they continue to be oppressed within it. Most contributory history is celebrative and has a definite morale raising function in relation to the present. There is, of course, the danger even in such contributory studies that the new history will remain essentially compensatory and uncritical. For one thing, the movement in question, and its significance for a history of women, is taken for granted. Women are seen as contributing to something that exists/existed independent of them. Further, their "contributions" are often analysed and judged not according to their value or importance for women, but according the their "use" for the movement in question. Renu Chakravarthy's *Communists in Indian Women's Movement 1940-1950*, (New Delhi : PPH, 1980) is an example of contributory history that remains uncritical. The book is a treasure house of information and of narrative accounts that are otherwise difficult to find. The refrain that runs through her account of women in the Telengana Movement is that she "fought the Razakars and the Nizam's police and later on the Indian Army, *standing shoulder to shoulder with* their menfolk." (p. 124-5, my emphasis, Compare also pp. 127, 129, 130, 132, 140 and so on.) The account moves from one major battle to another, telling us "old people and women and children were supplying stones and slings to their menfolk." (p. 125) ; or that "the women would surround the lorries and would not allow them to proceed, demanding that the men be set free." (p. 127); or that "women stood behind them (the men)" (p. 129); or that Swarajyam and Arutla Kamala Devi "even" fought with rifles (p. 130). The implicit acknowledgement of men as central and male action as norm apart, it is quite evident that this history is finally what the text itself admits to : a tally of the ways in which "the Telangana Struggle got sustenance from different sections of town and country people." (p. 135) In other words, it is an account, not so much of communists in the women's movement, as of women in the communist movement.

Not surprising, for the limits of the author's understanding of the women's movement are explicit. "In this great struggle", she writes of Telangana, "Women showed their fortitude and in the process liberated themselves from feudal chains that had bound them down for centuries." (p. 135) There is no room for problems or questions here, and the monotone of conviction rings through the authorial narrative. Which is probably also why she can quote Lenin's 1921 dictum with such approval in the introduction. "The Bolshevist Soviet Revolution", Lenin claimed "is eradicating the oppression and inequalities of women more thoroughly than any other party or revolution in the world has dared to." (p. 3). But neither in Chakravarthy nor in Lenin do we find out awareness that a revolution for women demands a change that is qualitative and not merely quantitative.

Take for example a very important (for women) campaign that Chakravarthy documents. Amidst all the accounts of pitched battle and of death that scar these pages in one description of a Sangam initiated action to get the local authorities to construct lavatories for women. Though the author admits that it was one of the "biggest and most popular' campaigns and that it "immensely popularised the Sangam" with women, it is given to us as an example of the "small and trifling", "local" (p. 138) problems that the Mahila organisers had to deal with. Nowhere in this account is there the awareness, let alone an appreciation, of the new sites for struggle or the new forms of political behaviour that emerge in the battle against women's oppression. Patriarchal norms and categories continue to haunt such accounts (as they do women's self conceptions). Rarely do we achieve the recentering of knowledge that a women's history demands. But the very fact that in contributory history women are now considered as a group and not as separate individuals as well as the awareness, common in such histories, that women of different classes were involved in different activities and contributed in different ways, make it an important advance in women's historiography.

P. Sundarayya's chapter on women in *History of Telangana People's Struggle* (Calcutta, 1972) can also be classified as a contributory history, though it is in many ways quite different from Chakravarthy's account. His is the most careful account we have of women in the movement. As one might expect it records in some detail the resilience, the selflessness and the heroism of women who fought in the squads or rose to positions of importance in the organisation. He tells of the courage of women who provided shelter, suffered in the repression and sacrificed their lives for the cause; he writes of sisters, wives and mothers, who supported the men in the family and moved into the Party and of hundreds of women who were part of the resistance. The list of 'martyrs' includes 20 women who were raped and killed. It is not an exhaustive record, neither does it claim to be one. But it does give us a sense of the range and quality of what women were perceived as doing for the movement. As important as the specific documentation, I believe, is the tone in which the account is given. One cannot miss the warmth and the obvious pride with which he speaks of these fellow fighters.

In no sense can we regard Sundarayya's documentation a full-fledged women's history but what gives the account distinction is the critical dimension that emerges through the narrative. Here we get not only the celebration of women's contributions but the awareness that women did have special difficulties that the organisation was not able to deal with. Unlike most of the other leaders we interviewed, Śundarayya, is conscious that the party did not respond to the enormous challenge women posed—and just as important—he regrets it. Take for instance this comment : "when we asked our squads, when so many women are coming to you, why did you not organize them into women's organisations, they answered that most of the women were mothers with children and as such it was difficult to recruit them into women's organisations that could effectively function." (p. 514) The excuse hangs limp and obviously does not satisfy Sundarayya any more than it does us, though there is no real critique in his account of the way the question of children and of reproduction is simply transposed into the problems of women.

The account also includes a long extract from a letter written by Narasamma, a young woman from a poor peasant family who we are told "joined the squads in 1950 and was an active cadre with good initiative, tried to carry out the tasks allotted to her by the Party and sought ways and means to accomplish them successfully. She tries to explain things to the people in her own simple way. She attracted the people and kept up their interest and respect. She had great confidence in the Party. She read and made efforts to develop the cadre." What follows is an extract from a letter she wrote to the party a crucial document for a women's history of the movement. Sundarayya obviously regards the comments Narasamma makes trenchant. She writes "during the Nizam-Razakar period, we tried to do everything and did not develop people's initiative to do things on their own though they were moving on a big scale.

The habit and practice continued after the Union armies came and we justified it saying that the people could not move because of repression, so we must ourselves do the tasks even if the people did not participate." It continues : "you must coach up cadres properly, even if it means a few more days' delay, so that they can go to the villages with a clear understanding. Especially you must coach them as to how to escape the enemy. With regard to cadre protection, enough precaution and care is not being taken. You must give us books which we can understand. You must take more pains to find such material for us."

Later, "we women are still being looked upon with the old outlook, that we are inferior. Any slip or mistake we commit, our leaders come down very heavily on us. It becomes a subject of open gossip and scandal. We must be guided and improved and not derided. If we move a little freely, we are watched with suspicion. Why have you not allowed any women to participate in actual guerrilla raids on the enemy?"

It is significant that Narasamma's observations about the continued surveillance, the harassment of women and the double standards that prevailed go hand in hand with her strikingly articulate statements about the vital need for education and democracy even in the thick of the battle.

Sundarayya often acknowledges that the organisation may have taken decisions that were too harsh : "Comrade Padma" was asked to give her baby away so that her husband could go to the forests – which means that she would also have to go underground. "I had always nursed a feeling of guilt after that suggestion of mine, "he writes "could I not have taken the mother and her two children some other place where Padma could have lived with her husband and children after his return ? At that time, we were thinking of years of armed struggle, till we achieved final liberation. All who were capable went to the forests, and others were to settle in jobs and places to search out new sources of living and do whatever they could for the cause of revolution ! ...But the Telangana armed struggle was withdrawn within one year after this. It was raking in my heart......" (p. 353) Obviously the main sentiment here is pain at having broken up the family and separated the parents from the children. But though we admit we might be reading too much between the lines, there is also the sense that the whole question of children (indeed, I would say, the whole question of sexuality and reproduction) had not been addressed adequately. And that was a grave omissions in such a movement.

A history of this kind obviously goes beyond a compensatory history. But as we pointed out earlier, the movement still stands in the foreground of inquiry and acquires a solid positivist weight. It is regarded as an objective fact, not a human event. Women are not seen as making history, or as having shaped the movement, only as having contributed to it. The ways in which women were affected by the movement, their struggles for survival and the growth (or the stunting) of their consciousness, are nearly always depoliticised even when they are not ignored. Earlier we quoted Narasamma's incredibly astute comments about organisational priorities and about the harassment of women. In Sundarayya's history (as in the movement itself, no doubt) these statements are quoted, but not seriously absorbed into the analysis of the movement. Rather, they are somewhat patronisingly recorded as the women's personal accomplishment not so different from being able to play the Veena, or having come first in class. "I have given this long extract, "he writes" just to give an idea of how women cadre were feeling and developing." (p. 348). Comrade Padma's problem—of children—was among the major problems for the struggle. Yet in the discussion it is diluted into a moral problem, a guilt at having violated family happiness. Once again there is no analysis that focusses on it as a political issue that had to be addressed if the movement was serious about women.

If these best attitudes were blighted by a patronization that effectively discussed them, it is little wonder that women often felt used and then cast aside. Or that, despite the pride we commented on, there was also the brooding pervasive sense that women were "problems." And as long as the "problem" was not politicized, as long as its dimensions were not rationally encountered, its contradictions acknowledged, it obviously remained, like other such problems, an embarrassment, accompanied by the barely articulated, but powerful wish that it would just go away—A wish that emerged not as much in explicit statement as in the small everyday moments of dismissive encounter whose corrosive power women anywhere will recognise. But for us today there is also the cold sweat when we think of what happened to women as a result, and how little, despite the enormous effort we have record of in the autobiographical accounts, things have changed. One is humbled, held in awe, by what Pramila Tai calls, "the sheer will power," the mental and psychic strength of women who came, who persisted, and who worked in the face of this.

On the fact of it, our study is also a contributory history. Who were the women who participated in the Telangana People's struggle, what did they do, what are their experiences, what happened to them when the struggle was withdrawn, where are they today, we ask. Yet there is a crucial difference. Our study embodies a shift in point of view that initiates the movement towards a women-centered perspective. What is history like, we ask, when it is seen through the eyes of women and judged by the values they define, what were their experiences, what was the movement for them ? The task obviously requires new concepts and new categories, but it also demands that we locate new sources and fashion new methodological tools. There was some documentary evidence we could draw on—a few references in newspapers and party documents, odd entries in police records, but hardly anything that would recover a history of women on the scale that would do the subject justice. What we did have though, were living voices that would help us recreate the past as women themselves has experienced it. The new information gleaned by word of mouth gave us a more accurate idea of (the grossly underestimated) *extent of* women's participation. But the real value of these oral testimonies lies in their ability to capture the *quality* of women's lives. Through them we are able to document experiences that traditional history would have ignored or even dismissed, to appreciate the issues as they appeared to the actors at the time, and set their responses and their struggles against the backdrop of that understanding.

In this history women are not spoken about, they speak for themselves. As listeners we have also to learn how to lay our urgencies temporarily aside and allow this emphasis on the *telling*, as against the *asking*, to emerge. Slowly, as we heard these life stories we began to build a sense of what the movement was for women; a sense of the pain, the isolation, the courage, the ingenuity, the creative brilliance of their lives.

What could be simpler, one might imagine, then asking those whose stories had not been told, to tell them. But we should never forget that speaking thus, from below needs courage. The women we interviewed were opening doors on their private lives, often drawing on areas of experiences that had never been exposed to scrutiny before. And in doing so they were challenging centuries of silence. Often one sensed, as one listened, (inevitably some, though by no means all, of the nuance and cadence of the spoken is lost in the written), how language had to be strectched to reach out to the as yet unspoken, and the still unspeakable areas of experience. We have to learn, as we read these life stories to listen for what another oral historian has called the "language of silence", straining to be heard. We need to understand the pauses, the waverings, the incoherence, the questions that are avoided just as much as we need to "hear" the real import of obsessive repetitions. When Dudala Salama returns with the urgency of a clock that must strike the hour to the pension that never came, she speaks not only of money, but also of a life that was given and vision that was betrayed. She speaks without the graphic directness of Priyamvada : "Our hopes were like an egg crushed in the hand," but as clearly and as disturbingly. Public or "Macro" history has an established language, a rhythm, a transparency that comes from being legitimate, uncontested, sanctioned by authority. In fact it is so powerful, that like ideology it has the capacity to distort the meaning of experience and blunt or even erase memories that go against its grain. We gradually forget what we are not allowed or encouraged to remember. In many of the accounts the struggle to capture and assert knowledge and experience that was in no way "public" or legitimate is evident. But we have to listen carefully to grasp and appreciate it. We need therefore to treasure and value the "little incidents" that survived the reductive balm of disciplined memory. When Pramila Tai tells us of the pain of being dismissed as a woman when she voiced a political opinion, or of her hurt when the Party refused despite the large number of contacts she had here to provide her shelter or allow her to stay in Hyderabad, these are not "mere details", but important pointers to dimensions of experience that had no public sanction. The accounts are open, exploratory, tentative. Yet once our ears are tuned to the subtler rhythms and the more searching implications of these histories, the monotone of public histories sound dull, even brash; their statements true but limited. For women's worlds however hidden they are, are meshed in with men's. And the insights they provide have radical implications for our understanding of a society comprised both of men and of women. For if we are to move towards the history of humankind and therefore to the possibility of its future, we need, not just to place women's history alongside that of men, but attend with humility and eagerness to the revaluations, reformulations and reorientation that it demands.

For us as a women's group searching out our past, oral history has a particular appropriacy. Though women have traditionally been marginalized in written cultures, they have always told stories. These are often, stories that uphold the norms of a culture. But they are also stories of those who resisted power and fought injustice. For each other, women have always had stories that never saw the light of the more public modes of patriarchal culture. Traditionally mothers pass knowledge and expertise down to their daughters verbally. Teaching and learning in this parallel culture is intimate, personalized, practical; the knowledge communicated nearly always about survival and resistance in a shared oppression. There were many moments in these conversations when we touched on these notes. Sometimes we were asked to switch the tape recorder off as the "still unmentionable" questions of (women's) politics were discussed.

Friends who read (the manuscript) these oral histories were surprised to find that the "major" "Public" issues of exploitation and repression hardly featured in these accounts. There seemed such a cleavage, they said, between the movement they had heard and read about, or even the history recorded in the introduction and what comes up in these oral histories. What does this mean, they asked. Did it happen because you did not ask them about it (in other words, was it a result of our biases ?) or does it mean that women were not concerned with these political issues? The comment is astute for it puts its finger right on the spot where certain crucial questions converge. Let us deal with the problem of our questions first. It is true that we asked, in the main for the story of their lives. We wanted to know about them and what they did, and we wanted the stories to emerge with the emphases that had came out of their own experiences. "Tell us about your life", we said, "start from when you were born, how you grew up, what things were like at that time, how you came into the movement and so on". We did not say, "tell us about the Telangana Armed Struggle". But while it is true history only answers the questions that are put to it, by no means follows that we get the answers we expect. Initially we too were surprised that we did not hear more about forced labour and the cruelty of the landlords, about *purdah* and rape. Rather we heard about problems with marriage and of brothers helping sisters leave the family and join the movement. We heard about relationships, about nurturing and child-bearing about their joys and their tensions as much or perhaps more than we heard about political action in the traditional sense. We heard almost nothing about planning or decision making, or of problems being discussed.

There are (at least) two factors at play here. One relates

to the context in which the question was asked. We did not when we set out on the interview, explicitly say, tell us about your life *as a woman*, yet we went as members of women's organisation writing a history of women in the movement. It was this orientation together with the emphasis on the personal, the subjective : "the story of your life", as against the public, the objective : "the history of the movement", that helped create this important change. (Almost unconsciously ?) they spoke to us as women about women in the movement. And as we sat together, and they talked at length in an atmosphere of informal intimacy, (the interviews sometimes took 3-4 hours) the areas that came into focus were those where we also began to realize a great deal of the politics of the women's question is actually located : the family. the policing of personal life and of sexuality, child-bearing, nurturing, relationships (with men, with other women), the movement as place of refuge, a "sanctioned" or "legitimate" escape from the confinement of the family and of womanhood, and so on.

It is difficult to believe that the women were not aware of the "public" issues involved. (Though, as other interviews with male leaders show, even for them the emphasis shifted in the thick of the struggle from issues, to battle tactics). But what becomes clearly apparent in the narratives is the whole parallel realm that absorbed women's efforts and their attention. It was a realm that lay outside the scope of political understanding at that time and consequently one in which they had to struggle alone, without a critical perspective. Priyamvada articulates it : "we were only individuals" she said. But that note runs through the other life-stories too. Here too women carried the "double burden" of a (largely unrecognized) private struggle tacked on to the public one. By and large this problem of the two struggles one visible, the other hidden continues to exist in party organizations even today. To say this, however is not to detract from the immense sense of "possibility" the movement did provide for the women the leadership chose to include—but that brings us to another dimension of the "private" struggle. We discuss that in the afterward.

As the theory and practice of socialist feminism today indicates, such a focus on the private might give us many more clues about the continuing vitality, not only of the structures that oppress women but of feudalism and capitalism, than debates on the law of value (useful and illuminating though these may be). We could go a step further. Our understanding of socialism too might be more penetrating and less abstract if we understood it thus from below, looking at its secret languages, its silences, its unarticulted values, its points of focus as well as the dissonances in its cognitive style, perhaps even the needs and desires it still nourishes, the substratum of fear and ambition it draws on. To what extent have these broken from the largely feudal moulds into which we are set? The scope of political understanding itself is enlarged, even changed as the question of women impinges on it.

Though oral history has proved an important source for women's, or for that matter, people's, history, we should not gloss over its very definite limitations. We generally tend to think of experience or memory or even the telling of a life story, as spontaneous and unmediated, concerned with the concrete reality of life and not with the abstraction of theory or the forms of fiction. But as anyone actually engaged in recording life-histories soon finds out, neither memory nor experience is exempt from ideological processing, what we remember is by and large, though not entirely, culturally sanctioned (even those memories we preserve in the secret recesses of our minds are ideological in that they are what is socially tabooed). Hidden conventions and models shape the "fictions" through which we grasp and project our lives. There is a striking awareness of this problem in Kamalamma's story. After one of the few extended accounts we have about the vicious forms of feudal oppression that was operative at the time, she declares "It was because of the Leninist Party... that I knew at least this much. My sister has forgotten everything". Kamalamma is aware both of the ideological filter that determined memory and the power of critical analysis to rouse and establish, what is, in relation to the dominant form, a counter memory. At sixteen Achamamba must have been one of the world's first barefoot doctors. She was barely literate, but she learnt how to treat illness, suture, clean and dress wounds, organise balanced diets out of the strange meats and vegetables that were available. She even attended to medical problems in the villages around. The medical and administrative knowledge she built up could well have provided a ministry of health with a model for our country. Yet her life story is composed mainly of bears and lions, attack and escape. The problem of sharing food satisfactorily finally appears more important than all the expertise she gathered. This is a problem we have to face. How do we evaluate women's work, when not just the official records, but the women themselves, continually make distinctions that devalue and marginalize their work ?

The question of experience has always been a thorny one for Marxism. The spirit of Marxism is critical and concerned with the totality of social relations, while experience (or so its critics would argue) privileges one point of view, ignoring the wider determinations at work. It substitutes desecration for explanation; it is not conscious of its ideological formation and so on. Yet there is no denying that experience speaks with warmth, a richness and a communicative power that no amount of cold analysis can susbstitute for. Further that it is finally the experience of the oppressed and the exploited which is never wholly absorbed by the ideological, that make action and change possible.

It is true that we have to be aware of the ideological context in which oral testimonies are produced. But this context is no more uniform in its determination than the oral history itself is. We can, as we argued earlier, hear the questioning, the hesitancy even the outright rejection of explanations as we read against the grain of the text's garrulity and listen for the gaps the hesitancies, the silences, the evasions. In other words, attend as much to what the stories reveal, as what they say.

But that is not all, this history creates a place (both politically and theoretically) where experiences that had no legitimacy on other accounts can be heard and their implications searched. Writing this history has been a process of discovery : not only of the limits of traditional historiography, but of the possibilities that emerge as we recentre our scholarship. There is for us as we think this question through, the knowledge that history as it is written now, may well turn out to be the history of a minority.

CHAPTER EIGHT

Special Address

DR. NEERA DESAI

Friends,

Let me at the outset express my great feeling of appreciation for making it possible to be here and I am sure my colleagues also voice the same , we have been very very happy attending and participating in this seminar or workshop whatever we call it. Actually after having a beautiful sight-seeing tour to come down to the Seminar is a difficult exercise but any way we have to do it. Now, what I thought after listening to two days discussions and presentations as well as yesterday evening's meeting with the students was that I should talk about the way in which some of the problems which have surfaced while researching or when I myself under-took some research problems or when I supervised the research of my students for M. Phil and Ph. D or when I collaborated with others or when we undertook joint research projects. So, though all these models and way of participation there are certain problems emerging and also certain concepts which I started in one way but when the projects developed and data started coming, the whole concept changed and the entire classification came through the empirical data. So I want to give a variety of illustrations and situations where certain problems can emerge and how one can tackle them.

Most of my colleagues have started with a small personal note on how they came to the discipline of women's studies research I also would like to fall in line and would like to say that I have no formal training as such in Sociology because way back when I did my B.A most of the jobs at that time required no specialisation for Sociology in the under-graduate level. So I had to take what was then a generally popular combination-history, economics, and that is how I under went my training in Social sciences. I did my M.A not in a formal examination but instead I presented a dissertation which was accepted by the Bombay University and that is how I got my M. A degree. So, at that time I did my first exposition on women because I wanted to study the "Impact of British rule on the Position of Indian Women". which was later on published as *Women in Modern India,* and I did my Ph D of course through thesis but at that time there was no course work involved. So I am a little unconventional and whatever known methodology and whatever known concepts of various empirical research which has evolved have come through experience , through teaching and also through self studies. This is my background and I have started my work on women since 1947 and it has been going on because I had a feeling that this was my field. Now before I come to the first empirical study let me tell you that from the subject of Sociology present here are Prabha and Malavika who are experts in the methods of sociology upto 1950s or late 40s. In India, in the field of sociology empirical research was not at all an accepted form of research. It was more that we were all brought up in the tradition of Dr.Gosil and Dr.Kapadia who in turn had done their studies in the historical analytical method and so the training in empirical studies or survey research as we call in Sociology has been much related and the craze. I could definitely use the word craze for survey research after fifties or after one would say the influence of empirical sociology, this is the background which I would like to share with you.

I am not talking about Women's Studies in particular for the moment, I am talking about the general trend in Sociology, the methodology which is more accepted is not only the survey research historical method but comparative method is also used, phenomenological approach and content analyses are the other methods employed. There are various ways by which the subject is being approached and so my plea would be that we should not be bound by empirical or survey research because it gives gateway to quantification. Quantification is very important, I think that the trend today both abroad and in our country which is growing is that all continue to use both qualitative and quantitative methods. Now this is a difficult exercise but one has to do in order to get a very cohesive picture. Now my first exposure is to survey research. Naturally I also grew up influenced by the survey research and the first study which I undertook was a "Study of Married Women Students in Bombay". I had taken to study married women in S.N.D.T University as well as Bombay University. We wanted to study the multiple roles they were expected to perform as a student, as a wife, as a mother and if she is also earning there is one more role conflict, multiple roles and all those various ideas connected with role, therefore I tried to study the multiple roles of this category of women. This is the middle class elite, because essentially I would like to tell you we do not usually get upper class girls, we either get students from middle class or lower middle class. Unlike Malavika, I would like to tell you that she has more from working class to middle class and I have more from middle class to working class. This has been my story of work and I want to revalue the middle class study. Some where in the new situation there is a need for this to be done. But right now my priorities are for this. Now one of the things which comes foremost is sensitiveness i e. one would say women's problems and women's expectation which came before me in these studies, when we had one question in the questionnaire relating to married women and maternity. Our problem was what kind of co-operation these women were getting from their husbands, mothers-in-law, fathers-in-law etc. But we were more concerned with husbands. because this is a closer relationship and also affects more. We had put all kinds of alternatives to know because they say that husbands are very co-operative. Then all kinds of alternatives when dissected show what kind of or what is the nature of co-operation at hand.

It could be taking care of children, taking leave at exam time, taking of notes for you because it is all related to the students role, looking after the household jobs or taking care of children etc. all these four or five alternatives were given. The last alternative which was given to them was congenial atmosphere and mind you, invariably as the forms started coming in, everybody had marked 'congenial atmosphere'. So now we were really surprised as we first thought that there was some cheating going by the investigator, she must be doing everything at home and simply marking like this. So immediately what I decided was that I must go back and have a sort of project to know whether they have gone to this place and whether the answers were correct or not and surprisingly enough for me the answers were correct because they had gone there and they all said 'congenial atmosphere'. Then because I was there face to face with them, I asked them what do you actually mean by congenial atmosphere, why do you say congenial atmosphere, then they said that, "we do not want our husbands to help us. Let them not help us, let them not do anything but atleast let them permit us to study". Now this gave me an insight into the expectations of women in the given context and this is also in a way corroborated by the fact and some other findings that you cannot in future realise that you can achieve something, your expectations become narrow and this I had one experience when I was doing neighbourhood study and the slum people when asked what kind of home they would like they said that we do not know as there is no chance of getting any home, so this is what the women of that particular period of time said, there were no action variable in terms of any other complete co-operation and were therefore satisfied with co-operation. Another insight which I got through the studies was the husbands conscience and what it is in order to see the other side of picture. We interviewed some husbands also because invariably in education, we have been told that higher education is the gateway to marriage and it is a waiting period till marriage is settled.

Some questions were posed to the husbands of the respondents of this study and here was another insight to the men's conscience middle class men declared that if their women wanted to spend the leisure time in studying and not doing anything else, we do not mind. So far as our requirements have been taken care of, they can do whatever they want in their spare time. Now, on the one side there is congeniality which is admired and on the other side there is no positive effort by the middle class men excepting the fact of permitting them to do a thing which they like in the leisure time. After the study was over, more and more questions began to occur in my mind with regard to some of the accepted sociological concepts. For example : role concept, role management and role adjustment. All these things I thought have been talked much more in terms either of men if in view or taking only one section of women. So this is the second insight which came to me about Sociology. We were talking yesterday about the whole concept of the family, we say that family has its tremendous influence on women ; women also have a very significant role to play for their family because marriage is a very important institution. Here is what I found when I went to the lower working class where I was making the study of women in working class that in the work and their families there was a study in collaboration. We had built a good deal of rapport with them and in one family there was one woman who was constantly telling us about the oppression which she was suffering at the hands of her husband. She would be earning but normally as it happens, the money is taken by the husband for drinking and he was also beating her. So at one point I asked will it not be possible for you to leave him ? You are earning so why don't you take the alternative and their reply was very very revealing of what marriage means and what family means; women say that when I stay in the family I have to face one wolf and when I leave him and go out there are hundred wolves waiting for me. The family is looked up more as a security rather than what we read in Sociology about family.

In contrast, this was hard reality and was something very very practical. The institution of family becomes the only supportive institution also came out in their study. Another thing which also sharply eroded all my concepts regarding socialisation and what the mother does to her children was also thrashed out in this study when we were talking to the Jhol women. In Bombay, we have tenements called Jhols where working class people usually stay especially factory workers. It is a *pucca* three or four storey building with a common bath room and passage, this is the topography of Jhol and it is identified with working class women. When I was talking with women about the whole socialisation problems as to understand whether they tell their children stories or not whether they sing songs to their children, do they gave some ideas with regard to rituals etc. to my utter surprise there was no such socialisation happening in the working class. Most of them say that we ourselves do not know most of the things so how are we going to give such things to our children.

CHAPTER NINE

Women's Studies in Andhra Pradesh: A Historical Perspective

DR. V. YASHODA DEVI

Women's Studies, a novel descipline in the world of education, has comparatively a belated origin, the brain child of National Movements and Women's Movements in the late decades of the 19th and early decades of the 20th centuries in the entire globe. In India, the Women had a glorious hoary past in Aryan Vedic times and their high status in home and society continued unabated but with some imposed restrictions till the Muslim occupation. They slowly and steadily lost their position of primacy, for the menfolk, in their fear of pollution, and anxiety to safeguard and preserve their pristime purity-racial, religious and progeny, developed the tendencies to confine their women to home, and enforced the veil-purdah in public to prevent the gaze of the ruling race—the Muslims. The Muslim expansion as far as Madurai in South India, dislocating the Hindu Kingdoms—the Yadava, Hoysala, Kakatiya and the Pandya, and establishing vice-royalties at Devagiri, Warangal and Madurai, convulsed everything that was Hindu, and obviously women were the worst hit and suffered abominable oppression. The rare instances of a Razziya Begum and Rudramadevi were exceptions.

By mid 14th century, the Hindus were wakened from their lethargic trauma and out of their concerted efforts, evolved the Hindu revivalist Kingdoms—the Gajapatis, the Reddis and the Rays of Vijayanagar, Contemporary inscriptions say figuratively that the earth immersed in the ocean by the deluge of the Yavanas had been rescued by Lord Vishnu as Varaha. The revitalisation of polity and society had taken place under the able stwardship of saints—Vidyaranya and new, vigorous Hinduism, on par with Islam was the established result. The women, from their previous role in oblivion, heaved a sign of relief on the revival of Hindu Dharma and Culture by the fresh kingdoms. In the Moghul rule till Auragazeb rather tolerant than the fanatic Sultanate, the Bahmanis were replaced by the five successive states and Madurai by the Nayaks, the feudatories of Vijayanagar Empire. Women had their participation in administration, public life and private sector, somewhat relaxed, than in the early medieval times. Women warriors, wrestlers, poetesses, orators, donors, philosophers are heard of in multitudes. The Vijayanagar expansion witnessed the glory of Hinduism in totality, as the Golden Age of the Guptas and it could withstand the bigotted policies of Aurangazeb and the Deccan Sultanates. While in the South, the Nayaks were the custodians, in the north the Marathas took on the torch and kept aloft.

The gradual infiltration of the Europeans for trade and contacts with Hindu and Muslim states finally leading to British expansion and colonial rule, had again disrupted the progressive trends among the Hindus for apprensions of fear due to the missionary activities of the Christians carried on mass scale. But the educational institutions attracted the attention of men who with confidence, influenced by the Victoria proclamation and non-interference with religion, and the religious and social reform Movements, allowed their women and children to resort to their normal activities. Women of upper strata, some as members of families in service of the colonial government had to mingle with the women of European families, and learn modern etiquettes, English language, etc.

Elite among women started women's associations. Women's Movements took to spreading consciousness awareness and awakening among the urban and rural female population and

attempt to eradicate deep rooted social evils and religious superstitions. When the Freedom Movement absorbed the earlier movements for achievement of Independence, Mrs. Besant and Mrs. Margaret Cousins had a major role with sizable segment of women following, and in the Gandhian leadership, women contributed substantially in the multifacetted nonviolent Satyagraha Movement. They aimed at the resurgence of Indian women as free individuals on equal terms with men.

Andhra Pradesh – Historical studies, an imminent dimension of Women's Studies aiming at gender equality and gender justice, would exert to achieve the goal by delving into the past by a methodical study of the source material available and arrive at rational conclusions, which would constitute the basis for the moulding of women's lives to become more vibrant retaining the fundamental Dharma i.e. Family. This implies the equipment and courage of women to challenge and overcome the traditional social and religious inhibitions at home and outside to prove that they are no longer parasites on man.

For a comprehensive study of woman in the ancient period in Andhradesa, a wider area than Andhra Pradesh, archaeology, as for any other region in India, is the main source, with literature serving as the secondary source. As the state formed part of Dandakaranya, several spots are celebrated to this day connected with Ramayana, proving Aryan expansion to the South, retaining the name of Sita in plurality from Vijayanagaram to the Godavari; Kadapa area is called the mound of Surpanakha, the sister of Ravana, instrumental in his abduction of Sita. Invariably, girls, till recently were given the names of Sita with its variants and Draupati in some communities. Places connected with the Pandavas are shown near the Godavari at Rajahmundry. Women of the Andhra Satarahana Empire (mid 3rd century BC to Mid 3rd century AD) could be studied with the tools-inscriptions rock, pillar and cave – with literary works, and Magadhan inscriptions as corroborating evidence. A knowledge of Prakrit, the lingua-franca of the age of Sanskrit, is required for a study of the inscriptions and King Hala's Gathasaptasati and the Mahapuranas. Women, in this age, as in the Vedic, had unrestrained comfortable and contented lives, distinguishing themselves in different walks of life. Among royal women were royal mothers, queens, and princesses who in their own right issued edicts recording building of Buddhist Stupas and Viharas, with attached Mathas to them and substantial donations for their maintenance for posterity. They participated in learned public assemblies. Gathasaptasati in 700 stories covers the entire spectrum of contemporary social life—women engaged in their household duties—grinding and pounding, singing songs, pastimes as playing ball etc. Their costumes, hair styles, ornaments, perfumery which are described in the work and could be verified by the study of the marble panels of sculptures of the Amaravati stupa, now in London and monuments at the Buddhist centres from Salihundam, Ghantasala Bhattiprolu etc. This was the Golden Age of Women in Andhra Pradesh, contemporaneous with the early Sangam Age in Tamilnadu.

For the post-Satavahana period upto the Eastern Chalukya Age (mid 3rd to mid 7th century A.D), Ikshvaku inscriptions, copper plate grants of the early Pallavas, Brihatpalayanas, Salankayanas and Vishnukundins and epigraphs besides coins are the main source, though the Mahapuranas, recorded and oral traditions supply the supporting evidences. Women's position in this period had become somewhat circumscribed losing its glamour and prestige compared to the Satavahana Age Receeding from political participation, women confined themselves to religious and social avocations. The Ikshvaku royal ladies and women of higher strata in society developed religious bent of mind than secular, and beautified the Buddhist monuments at Nagarjunakonda, who preserved on Nandikonda due to efforts of Dr. R. Subramanyam, and building of several viharas in Andhradesa Mahayana Buddhism had reached high watermark in this period and as Sanghamitra to Sri Lanka,

Andhra traders and missionaries from Amaravati proceeded on sea-borne voyages to distant lands, paving the way for the settlement of colonies and establishment of Brahmin dynasties of Kaundinya and Kasyapa to mention a few, in South East Asia, deserving the name greater Andhra. Temples to Hindu pantheon of Gods, originating from the Buddhist stupas, were raised by the Salankayanas and the Vishnukundins, e.g. Mogalrajapuram near Vijayawada. The change from Buddha worship to Bhagavata cult and adoration of Vishnu and Siva with their attendant deities is seen from the nomenclature and titles of the ruling dynasties, besides monumental structures of temples. Women play larger role in the subsequent age of the Chalukyas and Chola-Chalukyas (mid 7th to mid 12th).

The Chalukya age has a bumper of archaeological sources-plethora of copperplate inscriptions, with rings impressed with seals, thousands of epigraphs, and several temples—mostly in the coastal areas in the distinct Eastern Chalukyla style of architecture, and abundant coinage. The major literary source, the Andhra Mahabharata was rendered partly by poet Nannaya of the court of Rajaraja the Great, the last ruler of the dynasty of Rajamahendravaram. With beginnings in the 5th century Andhrabhasha – Telugu language, and literature made remarkable progress as seen from verses and prose portions in records. Foreign accounts Fahien and Hiuen Tsang help us in portraying the women in this age. They breathed more freely than in the previous period, with less restrictions as 'protection' imposed on them by male Chauvinism. Possibly, the spread of Sankara's Advaita enthused them, besides the prevalence of safety, securing, peace and prosperity in the country. to step out of their abodes and indulge themselves in socio-religious activities of building temple, and making sumptuous donations to promote learning, and arts of music, dance and poetry. A study of the sculptural wealth of this age will help to determine the life style of women and the impact of their counterparts in the neighbouring states of Tamilnadu and Karnataka on them. A good knowledge of Sanskrit and Telugu and architectural patterns is essential for the study of women's role in this period.

Medieval Andhra has two divisions the Kakatiyas, the Eastern Gangas and the Chalukya Cholas with mutual conflicts in the early part for expansion (mid 11th to the quarter of the 14th century) and in the later half, the Reddis, the Velamas engrossed in bi-lateral conflicts and with the Rayas and the Gajapatis and the final suzerainty of the Rayas by the 16th century with their Nayak feudatories safeguarding Hinduism. The plurality of emergent subsidiary dynasties, defacto independent though not dejure, was a significant feature of the early medieval period; their contribution in veriegated aspects was perpetual. The mutual matrimonial alliances for three generations of the Andhra Chalukyas and the Tamil Cholas led to blooming Chalukya Chola Empire under Kulottunga I. With the spread of Vaishnavism, and immigrants from Tamilnadu consequent on expeditions of conquest beyond Mahendragiri substantial sizeable Tamil settlements were established in Andhradesa, mostly in the Godavari region and beyond, composite cultural development is witnessed in the nomenclature of Vizag as Kulottungacholapattana, Bezwada as Jananathapura, Ghantasala as Cholapandyapura, Motupalli as Desiyakkondapattana and Kottapattana as Kollitturai. Women had no seclusion in this period and had their share in literary, and cultural development.

The age of the Kakatiyas, the second glorious period in the Andhra history was most formative, experiencing socio-religious revival, renaissance and revival of culture. The subsidiary dynasties, contribution to this development was significant. The Andhra temple architecture saw its climax in the Kakatiya style and Palampet temple is a worthy speciman. Sculptural exuberance, copper plate inscriptions, epigraphs in thousands, coins, literary output in the form of manuals in administration, dancing and on puranic themes in Sanskrit and Telugu, dramaturgy and musicology from the sources to be exploited by research scholars for an adequate study of women of the Age in their participation of various desciplines of progress. The first hand precious writing of foreign traveller Marcopolo and visit to Motupalle and his ecomium of Rudramadevi's rule is an important source. Rudrama's sister Ganapama Devi was the ruler of the Kota Kingdom owing formal alligiance to the Kakatiyas. Aravilli Nagamma popular as Nayakuralu was the Minister of the Palnadu Haiheya Kingdom. Renowned Machala Devi was a dancer in Prataparudra's court while Ganapatideva's court was a heaven of scholars. The Palampet dance figurines, most graceful and elegant attest for the high tones, the art reached. The common women's avocations could be studied from *Kridabhirama* and *Palnativira charitra*, popular as *Palansti Bharatam*, a miniature replica of Mahabharta war. Jayapa's *Nrittaratnavali* is an authority on the visual art of dancing.

In the later medieval period, there was a lull in the progress of women in martial arts but in administration and fine arts it was commendable. After liberation from Muslim rule after the Kakatiyas, the resurgent Andhra under Reddy dynasty, was hailed as *Mahitandhradesa* and *Mahaniyandhradesa* is the reign of Anavema. Though the architectural exuberance had a setback due to fear of Islamic vandalism, literature, drama, dance and music had their day due to healthy competition in their patronage by the Reddi rulers, the Velamas the Gajapatis and the Rayas of Vijayanagar. Women had full play for their talents as rulers, administrators, poets, dancers and musicians, besides household arts. Queen Anitalli exercised joint sway with her husband and independent rule from Rajahmundry, while Lakumadevi was the celebrated dancer of the court of King Kumaragiri. The annual spring festivals-*vasantotsavas*-at capital Sailapura provided the outlet for the people to witness the splendour of the kingdom in the profuse use of perfumes, imported from distant regions in North India and South Asia. Dance performances, dance dramas, music, concerts, learned discourses, gymnastics and pastimes were a fraction of these festivals. Motupalli was the international emporium of trade. *Kavisarvabhauma* Srinatha's works from a viable source for the political history and social life of the age along with the inscriptions, copper plates and epigraphs. Sanskrit commentaries by the royal scholars *Sangitachintamani* by Pota Komativema, *Kumaragirirajyamu* by king Kotayavema, several Sanskrit works —*Vemabhupalacharita* in prose by Vemana Bhatta, and works on polity by proteges of the Velama court of *Sarvajna Singabhupala* at Rachakonda and contemporary inscriptions, literature of Vijayanagar rulers should be studied for minute details of the many fold roles of women in this period.

Modern period falls into two parts—early modern and later modern. The predominant feature of the early period (AD 1600-1800) was the advent of the foreign merchants, starting of trade companies loyal to the Mughals and emergence as suzerain power by adoption of "Divide and rule" by taking advantage of the mutual struggles of the Moghuls, the Marathas, the Nizams and the Nawabs of Oudh and Karatic and the local Hindu rulers eg. Vizianagaram, Bobbili, and the Nayaks in the South. Women in this period, were mostly confined to their homes for "protection" from the forces of presbetarian fervour of the christian missions; English education and pollution of varying ways. This foreign phobia gripped both the Hindu and Muslim masses in the rural parts of Andhradesa. Inscriptions were not numerous, and Telugu literature had its heyday in Tanjore and Madurai, in Tamil Nadu new temples were few but village chronicles, *Kaifiyats* and *Sthalapuranas* and foreign despatches, give us a scanty portrayal of women of the age.

The next period (AD 1800-1947) witnessed the birth of Indian nationalism due to the discomfiture of the colonial rule, a retaliating phase of it leading to the Sepoy Mutiny, hailed as the I War of Independence (1857). The consequent queen's Proclamation, taking over paramountcy from the East India Company, guaranteeing non-interference with socio-religion of the people and full protection gave stability to them. With the exceptions of Rani Ahalya Bai, Lakshmi Bai of Jhansi, women were not yet still active, though there was some awakening in the masses in South India.

Indian nationalism, had received a form with the founding of the Indian National Congress (1885) and by the turn of the century, the Swadesi Movement, followed by the more momentous Vandemataram movement and on its heels, the

Home Rule Movement had strengthened it countrywide, Mrs. Annie Besant was the architect of the Home Rule Movement and her works as *India, a Nation* were timely and effective as a negation of the prevalent western nation that it was a conglomeration of races ever in mutual conflicts—an easy prey to colonialism. By this time, the religious and social reform movements had enthused women to understand their handships and awareness of attempts were on the anvil to better their condition, eg. raising the age of marriage, remarriage of child widows, spread of female education etc.

After the I Word War, the disappointed Indian nationalists became more anti-British and Mahatma Gandhi, with rich experience of non-violent satyagraha in South Africa emerged as the sole leader of the Indian freedom struggle with the wonderful weapon of satyagraha. Andhra was most loyal to the Mahatma, and women en masse-from children to very old mothers, responded to the clarion call of the Mahatma whom they considered as the incarnation of Krishna in the Mahabharata war. They, with devotion and sincerity, participated in the non-violent non-cooperation (1921), Salt Satyagraha, Individual Satyagraha and Quit India Movements—their numerical strength swelling from time to time. Women's participation in the constructive programmes—Charka propaganda, Harijan uplift, anti-liquor propaganda, foreign cloth boycott, Council entry etc. was greater and profound compared to the other southern states—Karnataka, Tamilnadu and Kerala. Sarojini Naidu, Muthulakshmi Reddi, Rukmini Lakshmipati and Durgabai Deshmukh were top rank freedom fighters from South India. The tremendous role of women in Andhra in the attainment of Indian Independence deserves to be highlighted.

For the study of women's multifarious roles in this interesting period, State Archives, Delhi, Madras and Hyderabad possessing the British records-despatches from the Presidency of Madras and Residencies of Indian States eg. Nizam, besides those in District Libraries, District Manuals and Gazatteers, encyclopaedias in English and Telugu, works on Freedom Movement eg. *Freedom Movement in Andhra Pradesh* (3 vols.) by M. Venkatarangiah, *Who is who in Freedom Struggle in Andhra Pradesh* (3 vols.) by Dr. Sarojini Regani and *High Lights of Freedom Struggle in Andhra Pradesh* by the same author, besides contemporary newspapers in Telugu—*Andhra Patrika, Andhra Prabha,* etc. and in English *The Hindu, Indian Express, Madras Mail, Swarajya* etc. give us some material. Patriotic literature, ballads, songs, dramas, speeches and traditional oral culture should be studied meticulously to cull out information for the activities of women in the long period. An indepth study of folk culture and mass culture will yield fruitful results.

Independent India—Women in India, possess equal rights with men, as per the Constitution. They are on par with their counterparts in the western countries, obviously on a higher plane than women in the under-developed countries. Women in Andhra Pradesh emerged quite bold, energetic, vibrant, strong and confident, as in the rest of India. Their participation in activities in public and private sectors—at State, National and International levels—both qualitatively and quantitatively so far is worth praising. Yet, much remains to be achieved at all levels particularly in rural areas. Contemporary indigenous sources—in archieves—State and Central, mass media, libraries, public and those attached to Universities and literature-prose, poetry, dramas—should be researched exhaustivly for a detailed and complete depiction of women's multi-dimensional activities and compare them with men and women in other States in India in their achievements. To assess, whether dejure status is becoming defacto status of women, a deep and elevated study on the part of women students committed to work for the descipline of historical studies is essential.

In contrast to urban culture rural mass culture should be probed thoroughly, for the study of development of women through the ages. Folk culture comprising folklore, folk songs, folk ballads, folk theatre, proverbs, adages, axioms, and sayings-some recorded but mostly unrecorded just transmitted by oral tradition through the ages should be collected from villages and studied. As man and woman, both hailing from woman, and together forming the human being, their intricate implications, mutual and in contact with nature—flora and fauna, hills, rivers and temples could be revealed from the mass folk culture and archival and literary. In the present age of tremendous technological advancement, women and children, due to tight activity of programmes in competitive life, have little aptitude or time to enquire or listen to epics or puranas highlighting the local and regional variations and interpolations or learn folk tales, or ballads eg. *Palnativira-charitra*, or Battle of Bobbili, songs celebrating seasonal festivals, and important events in the life of a female child-naming ceremony, attaining puberty and various phases of marriage and so forth. Neither the elder women have time for they engage themselves in viewing Television, listening to Radio Broadcasts or attending music concerts. So, oral communication between elderly women and youngsters is negligible.

For researchers on historical studies to proceed to rural areas, mingle with them to cull out unknown information from them with tact and patience, they must be provided with facilities and adequate funds. They must have a good knowledge of the local language and be able to elicit more information from the people than by the formal interviews with a few persons. Women's studies and methodology should be included in the curriculam of every educational institution—from school to university—not merely confined to women's colleges and universities. While the Padmavati Mahila University is job oriented, Mother Teresa Women's University in Tamilnadu is Action Research oriented and is turning out laudable work, eg. the Department of Historical Studies headed by Dr. A. Suryakumari. A comparative study of folk culture of the Southern states will yield us a full statured portrayal of women of South India through the Ages.

INDEX